U0100529

大展好書　好書大展
品嘗好書　冠群可期

大展好書　好書大展
品嘗好書　冠群可期

中英文對照武學(3)

李壽堂 編著　　張連友 校訂

# 88式

# 太極拳

## 學與練

### 附VCD

大展出版社有限公司

# 88 式太極拳學與練
## Study and Practice of 88-form Taiji Quan

作者　李壽堂

Writer　Shoutang Li

翻譯者　北美意源書社

孫慧敏　姜淑霞

Translator　　Huimin Sun, Yiyuan Martial Arts Books. North America

Shuxia Jiang, Yiyuan Martial Arts Books, North America

作者李壽堂和張連友的練功照

楊雲峰演示的88式太極拳

# 前 言

　　88式太極拳是中國國家體育運動委員會，繼1956年公佈「簡化太極拳」之後公佈的又一套現代太極拳運動項目。

　　1956年，在國家體委工作的中國著名武術家李天驥先生會同有關專家致力於楊式太極拳的推廣工作。他們簡化了傳統的85式楊式太極拳的動作難度，保留了楊式太極拳的基本要領和套路結構佈局，改編成88式太極拳，並於1958年面世。88式太極拳的面世，受到廣大武術愛好者的歡迎，作爲一項群眾體育運動，它在很短的時間內就在全國開展起來，特別是在20世紀五六十年代這一困難時期，太極拳作爲一項特殊的體育運動項目，更是受到廣大人民群眾的青睞。

　　88式太極拳有如下優點：

　　1. 88式太極拳以在民間流傳最廣的楊式傳統太極拳85式爲基礎，既保留了楊式太極拳的基本要領和結構，又簡化了動作難度，易學易練，便於推廣。

　　2. 88式太極拳的基本動作特點是在楊式新架的基

7

礎上進行了改編，與傳統的練法有所不同。它符合社會發展的需要，重點突出了健身和醫療價值，淡化了攻防內容，做到了與時俱進。

3. 在演練的時間和速度上符合科學的要求，練一套大約需要20分鐘，充分發揮了健身和醫療保健的作用，對提高全民健康水準和人民精神素質大有好處。

88式太極拳的推廣已走過了50年的歷程。目前演練太極拳各式競賽套路和傳統套路的人較多，而練88式太極拳套路的人相對較少，特別是在年輕的一代中練88式太極拳的人不是很多。本書詳盡地介紹了88式太極拳套路，望能在全民健身活動中發揮其重要作用。

### 註：楊式新架

原「南京國術館」副館長李景林在1929年提出要在山東國術館全面開設太極拳班，以推廣太極拳。他請楊式太極拳一代宗師楊澄甫三次修定，由時任山東國術館教務主任的李玉琳演示，並徵求楊澄甫及其弟子武匯川、陳微明、褚桂亭的意見而形成的太極拳架，稱為楊式太極拳新架，有別於1934年楊澄甫定型的楊式傳統架。李天驥先生是李玉琳之子，其父子為楊式新架之楷模。簡化太極拳與88式太極拳就是在楊式新架基礎上改編而成的。

# Preface

The 88-form Taiji Quan is another modern sport issued by the Chinese Sports Committee after the simplified Taiji Quan was published in 1956.

In 1956, the famous Wushu expert Li Tianji, who was working in the Chinese Sports Committee at the time, and some other relevant experts committed themselves promoting the prevalence of the Yang style Taiji Quan. They simplified the traditional 85-form of the Yang style while retaining its basic principle and form structure. As a result, it was adapted into 88-form Taiji Quan, which was finally issued in 1958. This form of Tai Chi spread all over the country within a short period and became very popular among Taiji Quan enthusiasts. It was especially welcomed by the people in the late 1950's and the early 1960's, which was a tough time in Chinese history.

The merits of the 88-form Taiji Quan include:

1. The 88-form Taiji Quan was based on the widespread Yang style of the 85-form Taiji Quan, and retained its basic

principle and structure while reducing the difficulty, so that it is easier to learn, easier to teach, and easier to practice. Simplified from the widespread Yang style of the 85-form Taiji Quan while retaining its basic principle and structure, the 88-form Taiji Quan is easier to learn and to practice.

2. The main features of 88-form Taiji Quan was adapted from the new Yang style Taiji Quan, different in some aspects from the traditional one, and its functions of health preservation and medical value were enhanced, adapting to the needs of the modern society. With the original parts of attacking and defending omitted, it's now focusing on the health-improvement and the medical effect.

3. Approximately 20 minutes are needed to complete the form. The time and speed to practice 88-form Taiji Quan have been adjusted according to the scientific standards. It is very effective in improving both the physical and the mental health of the people who practice it.

88-form Taiji Quan has been practiced for about 50 years. Recently, however, relatively less people practice 88-form than those who perform and exercise other competition forms or traditional routines, especially among young people. This book explains the steps of the 88-form Taiji Quan in detail. We hope that everyone will benefit from this book immensely.

## Note: The new Yang style

In 1929, Li Jinglin, the deputy director of Nanking Association of National Arts, appealed for setting up Taiji Quan classes in the Shandong Association of National Arts in order to promote the Taiji Quan sport. He invited Yang Chengpu, the modern father of Yang style Taiji Quan, to edit the Taiji Quan form three times, which was demonstrated by Li Yulin, the dean of Shandong Association of National Arts (at that time). The new Yang style was formed after asking for suggestions from Yang Chengpu and his apprentices, Wu Huichuan, Chen Weiming, Chu Guiting and so on. Mr. Li Tianji is Mr. Li Yulin's son, and they both made laudable contributions to the new style. Both simplified Taiji Quan and the 88-form Taiji Quan were created based on the new Yang style.

88式太極拳
學與練

# 目　錄

# Content

88 式太極拳 學與練

# 88式太極拳套路拳譜

# 88-form Taiji Quan Spectrum

## 第一組

1. 預備式
2. 起 式
3. 攬雀尾
4. 單 鞭
5. 提 手
6. 白鶴亮翅
7. 左摟膝拗步
8. 手揮琵琶
9. 左右摟膝拗步
10. 手揮琵琶
11. 進步搬攔捶
12. 如封似閉
13. 十字手

## 第二組

14. 抱虎歸山
15. 斜攬雀尾
16. 肘底看捶
17. 左右倒捲肱
18. 斜飛式
19. 提 手

20. 白鶴亮翅

21. 左摟膝拗步

22. 海底針

23. 閃通臂

24. 轉身撇身捶

25. 進步搬攔捶

26. 上步攬雀尾

第三組

27. 單 鞭

28. 雲 手

29. 單 鞭

30. 高探馬

31. 右分腳

32. 左分腳

33. 轉身左蹬腳

34. 左右摟膝拗步

35. 進步栽捶

36. 翻身白蛇吐信

37. 進步搬攔捶

38. 右蹬腳

39. 左披身伏虎

40. 右披身伏虎

第六組

81. 上步七星

82. 退步跨虎

83. 轉身擺蓮

84. 彎弓射虎

85. 進步搬攔捶

86. 如封似閉

87. 十字手

88. 收式還原

## Group 1

1. Preparing

2. Opening

3. Grasp Bird's Tail

4. Single Whip

5. Lift a Hand

6. White Crane Spreads Wings

7. Brush Knees and Twist Steps—Left

8. Playing a Pipa

9. Brush Knees and Twist Steps—Left and Right

10. Playing a Pipa

11. Step forward, Deflect, Parry and Punch

12. Withdraw and Push

13. Cross Hands

## Group 2

14. Holding the Tiger back to the Hill

15. Grasp Bird's Tail Diagonally

16. Fist under the Elbow

17. Steps Back and Swirl Arms–Left and Right

18. Diagonal Flight

19. Lifting a Hand

20. White Crane Spreads Wings

21. Brush Knees and Twist Steps–Left

22. Needle to Sea Bottom

23. Flashing the Arm

24. Turn Body and Throw the Fist

25. Step forward, Deflect, Parry and Punch

26. Step up and Grasp Bird's Tail

## Group 3

27. Single Whip

28. Cloud Hands

29. Single Whip

30. Patting a High Horse

31. Separate Legs–Right

32. Separate Legs–Left

33. Turn the Body and Kick with Left Heel

34. Brush Knees and Twist Steps—Left and Right

35. Step forward and Punch downward

36. White Snake Turns and Protrudes its Tongue

37. Step forward, Deflect, Parry and Punch

38. Kicking with the Right Heel

39. Cover and Hide a Tiger—Left

40. Cover and Hide a Tiger—Right

41. Turn the Body and Kick with the Right Heel

42. Striking Ears with Both Fists

43. Kicking with the Left Heel

44. Turn the Body and Kick with the Right Heel

45. Step forward, Deflect, Parry and Punch

46. Withdraw and Push

47. Cross Hands

## Group 4

48. Hold a Tiger back to the Hill

49. Grasp Bird's Tail Diagonally

50. Cross Single Whip

51. Splitting Wild Horse's Mane—Left and Right

52. Step forward and Grasp Bird's Tail

53. Single Whip

54. Working with a Shuttle (4 Diagonal directions)

55. Step forward and Grasp Bird's Tail

## Group 5

56. Single Whip

57. Cloud Hands

58. Single Whip

59. Push down the Body

60. Golden Cock Stands on One Leg–Left and Right

61. Backword Steps and Swirling Arms–Left and Right

62. Flying Diagonally

63. Lift a Hand

64. White Crane Spreads Wings

65. Brush Knees and Twist Steps–Left

66. Needle to Sea Bottom

67. Flashing the Arms

68. Turn the Body and Throw Fist

69. Step forward, Deflect, Parry and Punch

70. Step forward and Grasp Bird's Tail

## Group 6

71. Single Whip

72. Cloud Hands

# 88式太極拳套路
# 動作詳解

## 88-form Taiji Quan Detail
## Explanatio Step by Step

## 第一組

### 一、預備式

身體自然直立，兩腳開立，與肩同寬，腳尖向前。兩臂自然下垂，兩手放在大腿兩側，掌心向裡，眼向前平視（圖1、圖2）。

【要領】

頭頸正直，下頦微收，全身放鬆。不可挺胸或收腹，精神要集中。

## Group 1

### 1. Preparing

Maintain a natural upright position. Open the feet at shoulder width, toes pointing forward. Arms are dropped at both sides of the thighs, palms facing inward. Look straight ahead (Figure 1, Figure 2).

### Key Points

Keep your head and neck straight and upright; keep the chip in; with the whole body naturally relaxed and mind concentrated. Do not hold breath or push the chest.

# 二、起 式

1. 兩臂緩緩前平舉，兩手高與肩平，與肩同寬，手心向下（圖3）。

【要領】

兩臂前平舉時，動作要輕緩柔和，不可緊張用力。

## 2. Opening

（1）Raise the both hands slowly to shoulder height and width, palms facing down (Figure 3).

### Key Points

When raising arms, move them slowly and gently; do not push too hard physically.

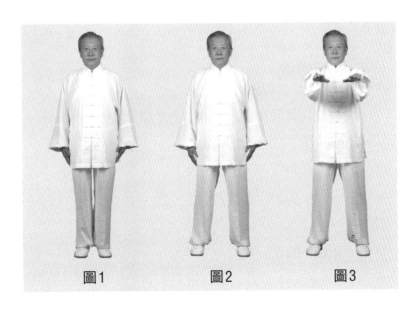

圖1　　　　圖2　　　　圖3

2. 兩腿屈膝下蹲，兩掌下按，兩肘下垂與兩膝相對，眼向前平視（圖4）。

【要領】

兩肩下沉，兩肘下垂，手指自然微屈。屈膝半蹲，鬆腰落胯，臀部不可凸出，身體重心落於兩腿中間。兩臂下落要與身體的下蹲動作協調一致。

(2) Bend legs slowly to a half squat (Ma Bu). Push palms down and sink the elbows to correspond with knees. Eyes look ahead (Figure 4).

Key Points

Sink the shoulders and elbows. Bend the fingers slightly. Bend legs to a half squat. relax the waist; Sink the hips. Do not push buttock out. The weight falls between legs. The pushing and squatting are coordinated.

## 三、攬雀尾

1. 右腳尖微向外撇，同時身體微向右轉，右臂平屈於胸前，左手隨上體轉動向右下方畫弧至右肋下，與右手上下相對成抱球狀，兩手心相對。身體重心落在右腿上，左腳收至右腳內側，腳尖著地，眼看右手（圖5）。

## 3. Grasp Bird's Tail

(1) Swing the left toes outward and turn the upper body to

the right slightly. Bend the right arm in front of the chest, palm facing down. The left hand follows the upper body to draw an arc to the lower right and stops under the right ribs, corresponding with the right hand as if holding a ball. Palms are facing each other. Meanwhile, shift the weight onto the right leg and move the left foot beside the right foot, with only the toes touching the ground. Eyes look forward (Figure 5).

2. 上體向左轉，左腳向左前方邁一步，腳尖向前，右腿自然蹬直，左腿屈膝，成左弓步。同時，左臂向左前方出（即左臂屈成弓形，用前臂外側和手背向前方推出），左手和前臂與肩同高，手心向裡；右手向

圖4　　　　　　　　圖5

右向下落於右胯旁，肘微屈，手心向下，眼看左前臂
（圖6）。

(2) Turn the upper body to the left. The left foot steps to the left front, toes pointing forward. Extend the right leg and bend the left knee to form a left Bow Step. At the same time, the left arm pushes outward. (That is: bend the left arm as a bow and push forward with the forearm and the back of the hand) The left hand and forearm are at shoulder height, palm facing in. The right hand draws an arc downward to the right side of the hip, palm facing down, elbow bending. Look at the left forearm (Figure 6).

3. 上體微向左轉，左臂平屈於左胸前，與肩同高，手心向下；右手經腹前向左畫弧至右（左）肋下，手心向上，與左手上下相對成抱球狀。同時，右腳收至左腳內側，腳尖點地，身體重心落在左腿，眼看左手（圖7）。

(3) Turn the upper body to the left. Bend the left arm horizontally in left front of the chest at shoulder height, palm facing down. The right hand follows the upper body to draw an arc to the lower right and stops at the left ribs, palm facing up, corresponding with the right hand as if holding a ball. Meanwhile, shift the weight onto the left leg and move the right foot

beside the left foot, with only the toes touching the ground. Look at the left hand（Figure 7）.

4. 上體向右轉，右腳向右前方邁出一步，左腳跟向後蹬伸，右腿屈膝，成右弓步。同時，上體右轉不停，至面向前方，右臂向前掤出，高與肩平，手心向裡；左手向左下落，置於左胯旁，手心向下，指尖向前，眼看右前臂（圖8）。

【要領】

（1）掤出時，兩肩下沉，兩臂均成弧形。分手、鬆腰和弓腿三者要協調一致。

（2）攬雀尾的弓步，兩腳橫向距離約10公分，

圖6　　　　圖7　　　　　　圖8

不宜過寬，也不能兩腳踩在一條直線上。

（3）左（右）腳收至右（左）腳內側。在動作熟練，下肢有足夠支撐力，並掌握身體重心變換要領時，腳尖可不著地，只須經過支撐腳內側向前邁步。類似動作與此相同。

(4) Turn the upper body to the right. The right foot steps to the right front, toes pointing forward. Extend the left leg and bend the right knee to form a Right Bow Step. At the same time, turn the upper body to face the front and push the right arm outward at shoulder height, palm facing in. The left hand draws an arc downward to beside of the left hip, palm facing down, fingers pointing forward. Look at the right forearm（Figure 8）.

### Key Points

（1）When pushing with the forearm（Peng）, sink the shoulders; move arms in arcs. The hands separating, waist re-laxing and bow step making should be coordinated.

（2）Feet are standing on the two parallel lines, which are 10 – 20 cm apart, not be wider than 20cm. Do not stand the feet on the same line.

（3）When move the left（right）foot beside the right（left）foot, only the toes are touching the ground. After the supporting leg is stronger, the toes do not have to touch the ground; it can pass the inside of the supporting leg and step forward. This rule also works for other similar movements.

5. 上體稍向右轉，右手隨即前伸翻掌向下，左手翻掌向上，經腹前向上向前伸至右前臂下方，然後兩手一齊下捋，即上體向左轉，兩手經腹前向左後方畫弧，直至左手手心向上，高與肩齊，右臂平屈於胸前，手心向後。同時，身體移至左腿，眼看左手（圖9、圖10、圖11）。

【要領】

下捋時，上體不可前傾，臀部不可凸出。兩臂下捋須隨腰旋轉，仍走弧線。右腳全腳著地，腳尖不可蹺起。

（5）Turn the upper body to the right slightly. Extend the right hand forward and turn it over to face down. Turn over the left hand to face up, move it past the abdomen to the upper front and stop under the right forearm, then pull both hands downward. Turn the upper body to the left. Both hands pass the abdomen and draw arcs to the left back until the left hand facing up at shoulder level. Bend the right arm horizontally in front of the chest, palm facing backward. At the same time, shift the weight onto the left leg. Eyes look at the left hand (Figure 9, Figure 10, Figure 11).

## Key Points

While "Pulling with Two Hands (Lü)", the upper body should not lean forward. Do not pull buttock out. The two hands follow the waist to move in an arc. The right foot should be entirely placed on the ground; do not raise toes.

圖9

圖10

圖11

6. 上體稍向右轉，左臂屈肘折回，左手附於右手腕裡側（兩腕相距約5公分），上體繼續右轉至面向前方，雙手同時向前慢慢擠出，右手心向後，左手心向前，兩前臂保持半圓。同時，身體重心逐漸前移成右弓步，眼看右手腕部（圖12、圖13）。

【要領】

向前擠出時，上體要正直，不可前傾。擠的動作要與鬆腰、弓腿相一致。

（6）Turn the upper body to the right, bend the left elbow and place the left hand to the inside of the right wrist. Turn the upper body to face the front. Push both hands forward slowly, the right hand facing backward, the left hand facing forward,

圖12　　　　　　圖13

arms rounded. Meanwhile, shift the weight forward, bend the right knee and extend the left leg to form a Left Bow Step. Look at the right wrist (Figure 12, Figure 13).

### Key Points

While "Push with Arm and Hand (Ji)", keep the upper body upright. The pushing hands, relaxing waist should be co-ordinated with bending the leg.

7. 左手經右腕上方向前向左伸出，與右手齊平，手心向下，右手隨即翻掌向下，兩手左右分開，與肩同寬。然後上體後坐，身體重心移至左腿，右腳尖蹺起。同時，兩臂屈肘收至胸前，手心均向前下方，眼看前方（圖14、圖15、圖16）。

(7) Move the left hand from the right wrist and extend forward to the height of the right hand, palm facing down. Turn the right hand over, so the palm is facing down. Separate the hands to shoulder width. Push down the upper body backward, shift the weight onto the left leg and raise the toes. Simultaneously, bend both arms to the front of the chest, palms facing lower down. Eyes look forward (Figure 14, Figure 15, Figure 16).

8. 上動不停，兩手慢慢繼續向後收，然後經腹前再向前向上按出，掌心向前，手腕高與肩平。同時，

身體重心前移，右腿前弓成右弓步，眼看前方（圖
17）。

圖14

圖15

圖16

圖17

【要領】

（1）向前按時，上體要正直，鬆腰，鬆胯。兩臂應隨著鬆腰、弓腿徐徐向前按出，沉肩垂肘。兩手須走弧線。

（2）攬雀尾整個動作均以腰為主宰。兩臂繞行須圓活自然。腿部的前弓後坐要靈活穩健。在做捋、擠、按動作時，後腿的腳跟不要隨意扭動。

（8）Continue moving the upper body, pull both hands back to the abdomen then press to the upper front, palm facing forward. Shift the weight forward, bending the right leg to form the Right Bow Step. Eyes look forward (Figure 17).

Key Points

（1）While pressing forward (An), the upper body should not bend backward, relax hips and waist. The arms should follow the waist and Bow Step to push forward slowly. Sink the elbows and shoulders. Both hands should be moved in arcs.

（2）The entire movement is led by the waist. Move the arms fluidly and naturally. Shift the weight steadily. When pushing or pulling, do not move the heels.

## 四、單　鞭

1. 上體後坐，身體重心逐漸移至左腿，右腳尖裡扣。同時，上體左轉，兩手（左高右低）向左弧形運轉，直至左臂平舉於左側，手心向左；右手經腹前運至左肋前，手心向後上方，眼看左手（圖18、圖19）。

### 4. Single Whip

（1）Turn the upper body backward. Shift the weight onto the left leg. The right toes are pointing the left front. At the same time, move both hands, the left one above the right one to draws arcs to the left. The left hand stops at the left side of the body, palm facing left. The right hand stops beside the left ribs, palm pacing upper backward. Look at the left hand （Figure 18, Figure 19）.

2. 身體重心再漸漸移至右腿，上體右轉，左腳向

圖18　　　　　　　　　圖19

右腳靠攏，腳尖著地。同時，右手向右上方畫弧（手心由向裡轉向外），至右側方變為勾手，臂與肩平；左手向下經腹前向右上方畫弧停於右肩前，手心向裡，眼看左手（圖20、圖21）。

（2）Turn the upper body to the right and shift the weight to the right leg. Place the left foot beside the right foot, with only the toes touching the ground. The right hand draws an arc to the upper right and turns into a hook in front of the right side of the body. The hook is at shoulder level. At the same time, the left hand draws an arc downward passing the abdomen, then to the upper right and stops in front of the right shoulder. The palm is facing inward. Eyes look at the left hand (Figure 20,

圖20　　　　　　　　圖21

Figure 21).

3. 上體微向左轉，左腳向左前方邁出，腳尖向左斜15°，右腳跟後蹬成左弓步。在身體重心移向左腿的同時，左掌隨上體繼續左轉慢慢翻轉向前推出，手心向前，指尖與眼齊平，臂微屈，眼看左手（圖22）。

（3）Turn the upper body to the left slightly. The left foot takes a step to the left front and pivot on the right heel about 15° to the left. The right foot pushes the ground to form a Left Bow Step. While the weight is shifted onto the left leg, the left hand follows the upper body turning over slowly and then push-es forward, palm facing forward. The fingertips are at eye lev-

圖22

el; the elbow is bent. Look at the left hand (Figure 22).

## 【要領】

（1）動作完成時，上體保持正直，鬆腰；右肘部稍下垂，左肘與左膝上下相對，兩肩下沉。

（2）左手向外翻掌前推時，要隨轉體邊翻邊推出，不要翻掌太快或最後突然翻掌。全部動作上下要協調一致。

（3）單鞭方向應稍偏左15°。

## Key Points

（1）While the movement is completed, keep the upper body upright, the left elbow is above the left knee. Keep the shoulders sunken, waist and hip relaxed.

（2）When pushing the left hand forward, the left hand follows the body and turns over. Do not turn the hand too fast or suddenly. The upper body should coordinate with the lower body.

（3）The single whip movement is directed 15° to the left.

## 五、提　手

右腿徐徐彎曲，身體後坐並向右側回轉，左腳尖裡扣，而後身體重心落於左腿。同時，右勾手變掌由右側移至臉前成立掌，指尖高與眉齊；左手收於右肘部內側，高與胸齊，兩手心左右相對。同時，右腳提

起落於左腳前，腳跟著地，成右虛步，眼看右手食指
（圖23、圖24）。

【要領】

（1）移動身體重心時，上體要平穩自然，臀部
不可外凸。在右腳跟著地時，右膝微屈，兩肩放鬆，
兩臂微屈，肘尖下垂。胸部肌肉放鬆。

（2）提手方向要偏右30°。

## 5. Lift a Hand

Bend the right leg slowly. Shift the weight backward and
turn the upper body to the right. Swing the left toes inward,
then shift the weight onto the left leg. At the same time, the
right hand changes into an open palm and moves in front of the

圖23　　　　　　圖24

face at eyebrow-height, palm facing the left. Bring the left hand inside of the right elbow at chest level. The two palms are facing each other. Meanwhile, lift the right foot and place it ahead of the left one with only the heel on the ground to form a right Empty Step. Eyes look at the right index finger (Figure 23, Figure 24).

**Key Points**

(1) While shifting the weight, the upper body should be steady and natural, do not push the buttock out. While the right heel touching the ground, bend the right knee slightly, relax the shoulders, bend the arms slightly, sink the elbow, relax chest's muscles.

(2) The direction of the raising hand is 30° to the right.

## 六、白鶴亮翅

身體向左轉，兩手向左下畫弧，在身體左側相抱，左手在上，右手在下。同時，右腳稍向後移，腳尖裡扣。

而後上體右轉，再微向左轉面向前方。同時，兩手隨轉體分別向右上左下分開，右手上提至右額前，手心向左後方；左手下按落於左胯前，手心向下，指尖向前。同時，身體重心後移至右腿，左腳移至體前，腳尖著地，成左虛步，眼看前方（圖25、圖26、

圖27）。

【要領】

完成姿勢，胸部不可前挺，兩臂上下均呈半圓形，左膝微屈，不可僵挺。身體重心後移和右手上提、左手下按要協調一致。

## 6. White Crane Spreads Wings

Turn the upper body to the left. Move both hands to the lower left to form an "X" at the left side of the body. The left hand is above the right one. Meanwhile, move the right foot slightly backward, swing toes inward.

Turn the upper body to the right then to the left slightly to face the front. At the same time, separate the hands. Move the

圖25　　　圖26　　　圖27

right hand in front of the face, palm facing left and backward slightly, fingers pointing up. Move the left palm slowly backward to the side of the left hip, palm facing down, fingertips pointing forward. Meanwhile, shift the weight onto the right leg and lift the left foot in front of the body, with only the toes touching the ground to form the left Empty Step. Eyes look ahead (Figure 25 – 27).

### Key Points

When the movement is completed, maintain an upright upper body; do not push the chest out; maintain the arms arched and bent slightly; do not be rigid. The weight is shifted in coordination with the moving hands.

## 七、左摟膝拗步

1. 右手從身體前方下落，由下向後上方畫弧至右肩部外側，肘微屈，手與身同高，手心斜向上；左手上提由下向上向右下方畫弧至右胸前，手心斜向下。同時，上體先微向左再向右轉體，左腳收回至右腳內側，腳尖點地，眼看右手（圖28、圖29、圖30）。

### 7. Brush Knees and Twist Steps–Left

(1) The right hand falls down in front of the body, and then draws an arc upward and behind the body to stop outside of the right shoulder. Bend the elbow slightly at shoulder level,

palm facing upward. Raise the left hand upward, then to the lower right, stop it in front of the chest, palm facing down. At the same time, turn the upper body to the left slightly, then to the right. Place the left foot beside the right foot, with only the toes touching the ground. Eyes watch the right hand (Figure 28 – 30).

圖28

圖29

圖30

2. 上體左轉，左腳向前偏左邁出，右腿自然伸直，左腿屈膝成左弓步。同時，右臂屈回，右手由身旁向前推出，掌心向前，指尖向上，高與鼻尖平；左手向下由左膝前摟過落於左胯旁，手心向下，指尖向前，眼看右手手指（圖31）。

(2) Turn the upper body to the left. The left leg steps to the left front, bending the knee and extending the right leg to form the Left Bow Step. Meanwhile, bend the right arm and push the right hand forward, fingertips at the nose level, palm facing forward, fingers pointing up. Move the left hand from the abdomen around the left knee to the outside of the left hip, palm facing down, fingers pointing forward. Eyes look at the

圖31

right fingers（Figure 31）.

## 【要領】

（1）右手推出時，要沉肩垂肘，坐腕舒掌，身體不可前俯後仰，與鬆腰、弓腿協調一致。

（2）摟膝拗步做弓步時，兩腳跟橫向距離不超過30公分。向前邁步時，如重心變換已掌握好時，腳尖可不點地而直接邁步，但邁步腳要經支撐腳內側向前邁出，此時上體要保持平衡穩定。類似動作，均可以此處理。

### Key Points

（1）When pushing the right hand, sink the shoulders and elbows; the wrist is sitting and palm is standing; do not move the upper body backward or forward. The hand pushing, waist relaxing and the Bow Step are coordinated.

（2）While making a Bow Step, both feet are standing two parallel lines which is apart no more than 30 cm. When stepping forward, if the weight is steady, the toes do not have to touch the ground, but it has to pause inside of the supporting foot then steps forward. Keep the upper body upright and steady. Other similar movement can be done in the same way.

## 八、手揮琵琶

右腳跟進半步，上體後坐，半面向右轉體，身體重心移至右腿；左腳提起略向前，腳跟著地，腳尖蹺起，成左虛步。同時，左手由左下向前上方挑舉掌，高與鼻尖平，掌心向右，臂微屈；右手收回放於左臂肘部裡側，掌心向左，眼看左手食指（圖32、圖33）。

**【要領】**

（1）身體移動要平穩自然，臀部不可外凸。沉肩垂肘，胸部放鬆。

（2）左手上起時，要由左向上向前，微帶弧形，不可直向上挑起。右腳跟進半步時要腳掌著地，

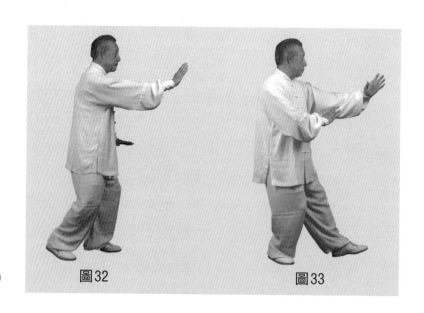

圖32　　　　　　　　圖33

再全腳踏實。

（3）身體重心後移與上體半面右轉、左手上提起、右手回收要協調配合，不可分解完成。

## 8. Playing a Pipa

The right foot follows up gently in a half-step. Turn the upper body to the right 90°. Shift the weight onto the right leg. Lift the left foot gently and move it forward with only the heel touching the ground to form the left Empty Step. At the same time, raise the left hand from the lower left to the upper front and stop at nose level, palm facing right, arm bent. Bend the right elbow and place the hand inside of the left elbow, palm facing the left. Eyes look at the left index finger (Figure 32, Figure 33).

### Key Points

（1）Maintain a steady and natural upper body; do not push the buttock out. Sink the shoulders and elbows. Relax the chest.

（2）While raising the left hand, the left hand should start from the left to the upper front in an arc. Do not raise the left hand straight. Place down the right foot on the ground with the forefoot first, then the entire foot.

（3）The weight should shift in coordination with the movement of the feet and the hands.

## 九、左右摟膝拗步

1. 右手下落，由下向後上畫弧至右肩部外側，肘微屈，手與耳同高，手心斜向上；左手由左上向右下畫弧放在胸部右側，手心斜向下。同時，上體右轉，左腳收至右腳內側，腳尖可點地，眼看右手（圖34）。

### 9. Brush Knees and Twist Steps – Left and Right

(1) The right hand draws an arc downward and behind the body and stops outside of the right shoulder. Bend the elbow slightly and the hand is at ear-height, palm facing upward diagonally. Move the left hand from the upper left to the lower right and stop in right front of the chest, palm facing down diagonally. At the same time, turn the upper body to the right; place the left foot beside the right foot with or without the toes touching the ground. Look at the right hand (Figure 34).

2. 上體左轉，左腳向前偏左邁出成左弓步。同時，右臂屈回，右手由右耳側向前推出，掌心向前，指尖向上，高與鼻尖平，左手向下由左膝前摟過落於左胯旁，眼看右手手指（圖35）。

(2) Turn the upper body to the left. The left leg steps to the left front. Bend the left knee and extend the right leg to form the left Bow Step. Meanwhile, bend the right arm and

push the hand forward from the ear, fingertips pointing up at the nose level, palm facing forward. Move the left hand from the abdomen across the left knee to the outside of the left hip, palm facing down, fingers pointing forward. Look at the right fingers (Figure 35).

　　3. 右腿慢慢屈膝，上體略後移，身體左轉，帶動左腳尖外撇；隨後左腳踏實，左膝前弓，身體重心移至左腿；右腳穩穩地收至左腳內側，腳尖可點地。同時，左手向外翻掌由左後向上畫弧至左肩外側，肘微屈，手與耳同高，手心斜向上；右手隨轉體向上向左下畫弧落於左肩前，手心斜向下，眼看左手（圖36、

圖34　　　　　　　　圖35

37、38）。

（3）Bend the right knee slowly. Move the upper body backward slightly. Turn the body to the left, leading the left toes to move outward. Place the left foot on the ground solidly, bending the knee. Shift the weight onto the left leg. Bring the right foot beside the left one with or without the toes touching the ground. Turn over the left hand and draw an arc upward and behind the body then stop it outside of the left shoulder. Bend the elbow slightly with the hand at ear-height, palm facing upward diagonally. The right hand follows the body to move upward then to the lower left and stops in front of the left shoulder, palm facing down diagonally. Eyes look at the left hand

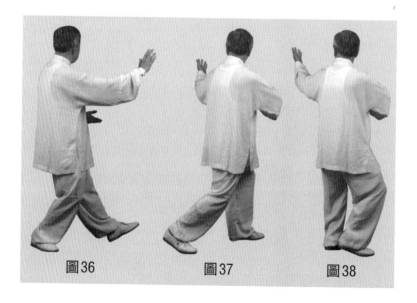

圖36          圖37          圖38

（Figure 36 – 38）.

4. 與動作2說明同，只是左右相反（圖39）。

5. 與動作3說明同，只是左右相反（圖40、41、

圖39

圖40                           圖41

42）。

6. 與動作2說明同（圖43）。

（4）Movement is the same as（2）, in the opposite direction （Figure 39）.

（5）Movement is the same as（3）, in the opposite direction （Figure 40 – 42）.

（6）Movement is the same as（2）（Figure 43）.

【要領】

右摟膝拗步與左摟膝拗步相同，只是左右相反。

## Key Points

The key points are the same as the former "Brush Knees

圖42　　　　　　　　　　圖43

and Twist Steps – Left", in opposite direction.

## 十、手揮琵琶

說明與要領均與前同（圖44、圖45）。

### 10. Playing a Pipa

The movements and Key Points are the same as the former "Playing a Pipa"(Figure 44, 45).

## 十一、進步搬攔捶

1. 身體左轉，左腳尖外撇再踏實。同時，左掌翻轉，左臂平屈胸前，手心向下；右掌變拳由體前向左下畫弧，至右（左）肋旁，拳心向下。此時身體重心

圖44　　　　　圖45

前移落於左腿，右腿微屈，腳跟提起向外扭轉，眼看左手（圖46）。

## 11. Step forward, Deflect, Parry and Punch

(1) Turn the upper body to the left, leading the left toes to turn outward. Then place the entire left foot on the ground. Meanwhile, turn over the left hand and bend the arm in front of the chest, palm facing downward. Turn the right hand into a fist to draw an arc to the lower left and stop it at the outside of the left ribs, the palm facing downward. Shift the weight to the left and bend the right leg. Lift the right heel and swing it outward. Look at the left hand (Figure 46).

2. 上體右轉，右拳自胸前向前翻轉撇出，拳心向上，左手順勢落於左胯旁。同時，右腳前邁一步，腳尖外撇，眼看右拳（圖47）。

(2) Turn the upper body to the right. The right fist punches downward with the back of the fist from the front of the chest, the palm facing upward. The left hand falls down to the outside of the left hip. Meanwhile, the right foot steps forward with the toes pointing right front. Eyes look at the right fist (Figure 47).

3. 身體重心前移於右腳，左手自身體左側向上向左再向前畫弧攔出，掌心向前下方。同時，左腳前邁一步，腳跟著地。右拳向右畫弧收至腰部右側，拳心向上，眼看左手（圖48）。

（3）Shift the weight onto the right foot. Move the left hand from the left to the upper left first, then forward to parry in front of the body, palm facing the lower front. Meanwhile, the left foot steps forward with only the heel touching the ground. The right fist draws an arc to the right then backward to the right side of the waist. The palm is facing up. Eyes look at the left hand (Figure 48).

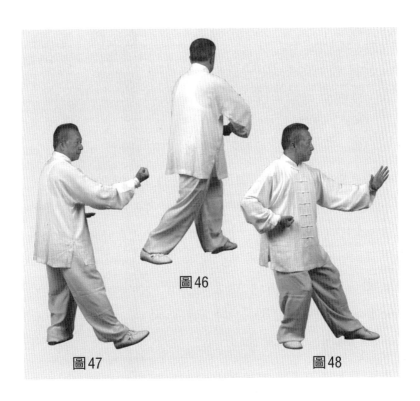

圖46

圖47                      圖48

4. 左腿前弓成左弓步。同時，右拳向前打出，拳眼向上，高與胸平，左手附於右前臂內側，眼看右拳（圖49）。

（4）Bend the left knee to form the Left Bow Step. At the same time, the right fist punches forward at the chest level, the eye of the fist facing upward. The left hand is inside of the right arm. Eyes look at the right fist (Figure 49).

## 【要領】

上體保持正直，右拳要鬆握。右拳回收時，前臂應緩緩內旋畫弧，然後再外旋挎於右腰側，拳心向上。右拳向前打出時，右肩要隨拳略前順，沉肩垂肘，臂微屈。弓步時，兩腳橫向距離不小於10公分。

## Key Points

Maintain the upper body upright. The right fist should not hold too tight. When moving the right fist, the forearm should be rotated inward first, then outward to the right side of the waist, the palm facing upward. When the right fist punches forward, the shoulder should follow the fist to lean forward slightly. Sink the elbows and shoulders. Arms are bent slightly. When practicing Bow Step (Gong Bu), the feet stand on two lines, which are not less than 10 cm apart.

## 十二、如封似閉

1. 左手由右腕下伸出，右拳變掌，兩手手心逐漸翻轉向上並慢慢分開回收至兩肋旁。同時，上體後坐，左腳尖蹺起，身體重心移於右腿，眼看前方（圖50、圖51）。

### 12. Withdraw and Push

（1）The left hand thrusts forward under the right wrist.

圖49

圖50

圖51

Change the right fist into an open palm. Turn both hands over to face upward and pull them to the sides of the ribs. At the same time, move the upper body backward; lift the left toes; shift the weight onto the right leg. Eyes look at the front(Figure 50, Figure 51).

2. 兩手在胸前翻掌，與肩同寬，向下經腹前再向上向前推出，手心向前。同時，左腿前弓成左弓步，眼看前方（圖52、圖53）。

(2) Turn both hands over in front of the chest at shoulder width and push them down to the lower abdomen, then to the upper front. The palm is facing forward. Bend the left knee to

圖52　　　　　　　圖53

form the Left Bow Step. Eyes look at the front（Figure 52, Figure 53）.

## 【要領】

身體後坐時須鬆腰、鬆胯，上體不可後仰，臀部不要外凸。兩臂隨身體回收時，肩、肘略向外鬆開，不可直線抽回。兩手推出時，寬度要略窄於兩肩。

### Key Points

When shifting the body backward, relax the waist and hips; the upper body should not lean backward; the buttock should not push out. When both arms follow the body pulling back, shoulders and elbows are relaxed towards out. Do not pull arms back in a straight line. When pushing forward, two hands should be apart a little narrower than shoulder width.

## 十三、十字手

1. 身體重心移向右腿，左腳尖裡扣，向右轉體。右手隨轉體動作向右平擺畫弧，與左手成兩臂側平舉，掌心向前，肘部微屈。同時，右腳尖隨著轉體稍向外撇，成右側弓步，眼看右手（圖54、圖55）。

### 13. Cross Hands

（1）Shift the weight onto the right leg and swing the right toes inward. Turn the upper body to the right. The right hand follows the body to draw an arc to the right until it is at shoulder level, palm facing forward. Swing the right toes outward, bend the right knee and extend the left leg to form the Right Bow Step (Gong Bu). Eyes look at the right hand (Figure 54, Figure 55).

2. 身體重心慢慢移於左腿，右腳尖裡扣；隨即右腳向左收回，兩腳距離與肩同寬，兩腿緩緩蹬直成開立步，腳尖向前。同時，兩手向下經腹前畫弧交叉合抱於胸前，兩臂撐圓，腕高與肩平，右手在外成十字手，手心均向裡，眼看前方（圖56、圖57）。

（2）Shift the weight onto the left leg. Swing the right toes inward. Bring the right foot close to the left foot apart at shoul-

圖54　　　　　　　圖55

der width. Extend both legs and stand up slowly, the weight sharing by both feet. The feet are parallel to each other, toes pointing to the front. Meanwhile, both hands draw arcs downward simultaneously and meet in front of the chest to form an "X". The right hand is on the outside. The arms are arched with wrists at shoulder level, palms facing the body. Eyes look straight ahead (Figure 56, Figure 57).

【要領】

兩手分開和合抱時，要保持上體正直，不可前俯。右腳回收時，腳尖先向裡扣。站起後，身體仍然正直，頭微向上領，下頜稍向內收。兩臂環抱時須圓

圖56　　　　圖57

撐，達到圓滿舒適，沉肩垂肘，空開腋下，不可夾臂。

## Key Points

When the hands draw arcs from either side of the body, the upper body should not bow. When bringing the right foot to the left foot, swing the toes first. When standing up, maintain an upright upper body; draw the head up; pull the chin in slightly. When the two hands cross in front of the chest, both arms have to be arched; elbows rounded; shoulders relaxed and sunken; the armpit is open; the arms should not touch the body.

## 第二組

## 十四、抱虎歸山

1. 身體重心微向右移，左腳尖向裡扣，然後兩腿屈膝，身體重心落於左腿。隨即身體左轉，左手由胸前向下向左畫弧至與左肩齊平，手心斜向上；右臂屈肘，右手回收至左肩前，手心斜向下，眼看左手（圖58）。

## Group 2

## 14. Holding the Tiger back to the Hill

（1）Shift the weight to the right slightly, and swing the left toes inward. Bend both legs, shift the weight onto the left leg and turn the upper body to the left. The left hand draws an arc from the chest to the lower left and stops at shoulder level, palm facing upward diagonally. Bend the right elbow and put the hand in front of the left shoulder, palm facing downward diagonally. Eyes look at the left hand (Figure 58).

2. 上體微向右轉，右腳向右後方邁一步，屈膝成右弓步。同時，右手隨上體繼續向右後轉體向下向右摟按於右膝外側；左臂屈肘，左手經左耳旁向前推出，高與鼻尖齊平，眼看左手（圖59）。

(2) Turn the upper body to the right. The right foot steps forward to form the Right Bow Step. Meanwhile, the right hand

圖58　　　　　　　圖59

follows the upper body to push above the right knee and stops outside of it. Bend the left arm and push it forward from the left ear at nose level. Eyes look at the left hand (Figure 59).

## 【要領】

由站立勢，身體重心先移至右腿，再裡扣左腳並屈膝半蹲。右手摟按時較「摟膝拗步」略高，然後落於右膝外側。轉身與推掌要協調一致，方向應為起勢右側偏後30°。

### Key Points

Start from standing straight. Shift the weight onto the right leg first, then swing the left toes inward and bend the leg in a half squat. When pushing forward, the right hand should be higher than that in "Brush Knees and Twist Steps" and stop at the outside of the right knee. The body turns in coordination with the hand's pushing. Direction is 30° to the right of the Opening form.

## 十五、斜攬雀尾

上體微向右轉，隨轉體右手從右下側上舉，與肩同高，手心斜向下；同時，左手翻轉，手心向上，落至右前臂下方，然後做捋、擠、按動作。方法均與「攬雀尾」式相同，方向同「抱虎歸山」式（圖60～圖65）。

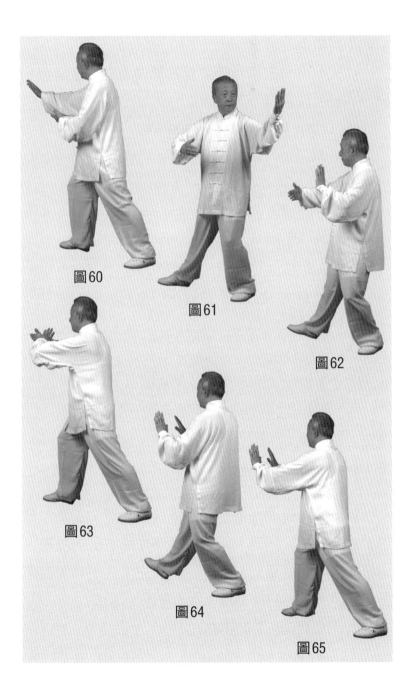

圖60

圖61

圖62

圖63

圖64

圖65

【要領】

此式除沒有的動作外，其餘都與「右攬雀尾」相同，只是面向斜角方向。

### 15. Grasp Bird's Tail Diagonally

Turn the upper body to the right slightly. Following the body moving, raise the right hand from the lower right up to shoulder level, palm facing downward diagonally. Meanwhile, turn over the left hand to face upward and thrust under the right forearm. Rest of the movement is the same as "Grasp Bird's Tail", in the direction of "Holding the Tiger back to the Hill" (Figure 60 – 65).

### Key Points

The key points are same as "Grasp Bird's Tail – Left". The only difference: direction is diagonal, and there is no "Push with Forearm" in the movement.

## 十六、肘底看捶

1. 上體後倚，身體重心慢慢移至左腿，上體左轉帶動右腳裡扣。同時，兩手隨轉體左高右低向左畫弧運轉，直至左臂舉於左側，手心向左；右手經腹前運至左肋前，手心向後上方，眼看左手（圖66）。

### 16. Fist under the Elbow

(1) The upper body leans backward. Shift the weight onto

the left leg gradually to lead the right toes to swing inward. At the same time, both hands follow the body and draw arcs to the left, palms facing the left. The left hand is higher than the right hand. Stop when the left hand is at the left side of the body. The right hand crosses the front of the abdomen and stops in front of the left ribs, palm facing upward and also towards the body. Eyes look at the left hand (Figure 66).

2. 身體重心再漸漸移於右腿，上體右轉，左腳收至右腳內側，腳尖可點地。同時，右手向右上方畫弧運轉至右側平舉，與肩同高，手心向外；左手也同時向下，經腹前向右上畫弧至右肩前，手心向裡，眼看右手（圖67）。

圖66                    圖67

(2) Turn the upper body to the right and shift the weight to the right leg gradually. The left foot steps beside the right foot, with toes touching the ground. At the same time, the right hand draws an arc to the upper right and stops at the outside of the body at shoulder level, palm facing outward. The left hand draws an arc downward past the front of the abdomen and stops in front of the right shoulder, palm facing inward. Eyes look at the right hand (Figure 67).

3. 左腳向左側偏前方向邁一步，腳尖外撇，身體重心向左腿過渡，身體左轉；右腳隨身體的轉動向左腳跟進半步，落於左腳後。同時，左手隨轉體向左運轉至身體左方再收至左腰側，掌心向上；右臂也隨轉體向左畫弧運轉，平屈於胸前，眼看前方（圖68、圖69）。

【要領】

邁左腳和兩臂的運轉要與身體左轉協調配合。左腿站穩，右腳再跟進半步。

(3) The left foot takes a step to the left front, swinging the toes outward. Turn the upper body to the left and shift the weight to the left leg. The right foot follows the body taking a half step and falls behind the left foot. At the same time, the left hand follows the body and moves to the left until it is at the

left side of the waist, palm facing upward. The right arm follows the body to the left and bends vertically in front of the
chest. Eyes look at the front (Figure 68, 69).

### Key Points

The left foot steps in coordination with the movement of
the arm and body. After the left foot stands firmly, the right
foot follows in a half step.

4. 左手由腰際經右手腕上面向前穿出，成側立
掌，掌心向右，高與鼻尖齊平；右掌則變拳置於左肘
下，拳眼向上。與此同時，身體重心落於右腿，左腳
向前邁出小半步，腳跟點地，膝微屈，成左虛步，眼

圖68　　　　圖69

看左掌（圖70）。

【要領】

身體自然正直，鬆肩鬆胯。左掌前伸時，重心在右腿，左膝要微屈，不可挺直。

(4) The left hand thrusts forward over the right wrist from the waist to form a Standing Palm, palm facing right, fingers pointing up at nose level. The right hand forms a fist, the eye of the fist facing up. Then place it under the left elbow. Meanwhile, shift the weight onto the right leg. The left foot takes a half step forward, only the heel touching the ground, bending the knee to form a left Empty Step. Eyes look at the left hand (Figure 70).

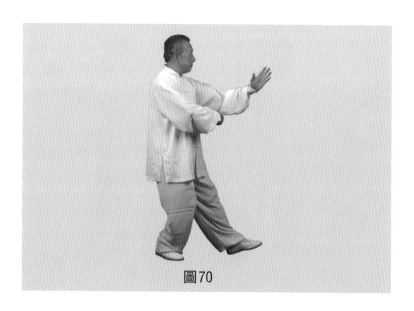

圖70

### Key Points

Keep the upper body upright. Relax shoulders and hips. When the left hand thrusts forward, the weight is on the right leg. Bend the left knee The left knee should not be straight.

## 十七、左右倒捲肱

1. 右拳變掌，手心轉向上，隨上體右轉經腹前由後下方畫弧平舉，臂微屈，左手隨即翻掌向上。左腿膝部放鬆，眼隨著上體右轉先向右看，再轉向前方看左手（圖71、圖72）。

### 17. Step Back and Swirl Arms – Left and Right

（1）Turn the upper body to the right slightly. Turn over

圖71　　　　　　　　圖72

the right hand to face up. The right hand follows the body to draw an arc past the abdomen and stops behind the body at head level. Eyes look to the back at the right hand. At the same time, turn over the left hand to face up. Turn the head forward to look at the left hand (Figure 71, Figure 72).

2. 右臂屈肘，右手由右耳側向前推出，手心向前；左臂屈肘後撤，手心向上，撤至左肋外側。同時，左腿輕輕提起，向後偏左側退一步，腳掌先著地，然後慢慢踏實，身體重心移至左腿成右虛步，右腳隨轉體以腳掌為軸扭正，眼看右手（圖73、圖74）。

(2) Bend the right elbow and push the hand from the out-

圖73　　　　　　　　　圖74

side of the right ear, palm facing forward. Bend the left elbow and pull the left hand backward to the outside of the left ribs. At the same time, lift the left foot and place the toes next to the right foot gently. The left foot takes a step backward with only the forefoot on the ground first, then entire foot. Shift the weight onto the left leg to form an Empty Step. The right foot follows the body, pivoting on the right forefoot until the toes point forward. Look at the right hand (Figure 73, Figure 74).

3. 上體微向左轉，同時，左手隨轉體向後上方畫弧平舉，手心仍向上；右手隨即翻掌，手心向下；眼隨轉體先向後看，再轉向前方看右手（圖75）。

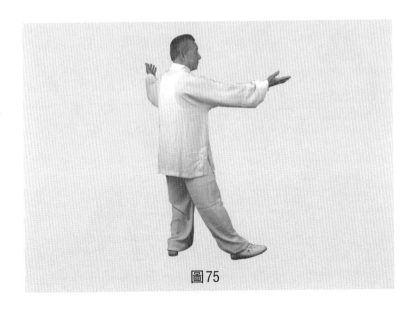

圖75

（3）Continue to turn the upper body to the left and move the left hand backward and downward to draw an arc, palm facing upward. Turn over the right hand face downward. Eyes follow the body to look at behind first, then the right hand（Figure 75）.

4. 與動作2說明同，只是左右動作相反（圖76、圖77）。

5. 與動作3說明同，只是左右動作相反（圖78）。

6. 與動作2說明同（圖79、圖80）。

（4）Movement is the same as（2）, in the opposite direction（Figure 76, Figure 77）.

圖76　　　　　　　　　　圖77

(5) Movement is the same as (3), in the opposite direction (Figure 78).

(6) Movement is the same as (2) (Figure 79, Figure 80).

圖78

圖79                    圖80

## 【要領】

前推手不宜伸直，後手也不可直向回抽，要走弧線。前推時要轉腰鬆胯，兩手速度要一致，避免僵硬。退步時，起腳要微上拔再後撤，並以前腳掌先著地，再慢慢踏實，同時前腳扭正。退步時，左右腳分別略向左右後斜一點落腳，避免成直線步和麻花步。後退步時要平穩，不可忽高忽低。虛步不可把膝部挺直。轉體動作兩眼要向左右看，隨前手翻掌再回頭看前手。

### Key Points

When pushing a hand, do not extend the arm straight. When pulling back a hand, do not pull it in straight line; move it in an arc and keep an even speed. Relax hips. Move the foot as pulling it out of the mud and step lightly forward. Step feet backward in an arc, forefoot touching the ground first, then the entire foot. The feet should not be lined up or intersected. Keep upper body stable, while moving backward; do not lift or push down the body. With the "Empty Step", the knee should not be stiff. Eyes follow the body to look at the left or right first, then, look backward while the hand turns over.

## 十八、斜飛式

1. 上體微向左轉，同時，左手向後上方畫弧平舉，手心斜向上；右手鬆腕，掌心斜向下。眼隨轉體先向後看，再轉向前方看右手（圖81）。

## 18. Diagonal Flight

（1）Turn the upper body to the left slightly. At the same time, the left hand draws an arc to the back right, at shoulder level. The palm faces upward diagonally. Relax the right wrist, palm facing downward diagonally. Eyes follow the body to look backward first, and then turn to look at the right hand (Figure 81).

2. 左手畫弧，左臂平舉胸前，左手心向下；右手經體前下方畫弧與左手上下相抱。右腳收至左腳跟旁，腳尖點地（圖82）。

圖81         圖82

(2) The left hand draws an arc until the arm is in front of the chest, palm facing downward. The right hand draws an arc under the left arm to form an "X" in front of the lower chest. Place the right foot beside the left heel, only the toes touching the ground (Figure 82).

3. 以左腳掌為軸，左腳跟後碾，上體右轉，右腳向右前方邁出，成右弓步，面向右前方。同時，兩手向右上左下分開，右手高與眼齊，手心斜向上；左手落於左胯旁，手心向下，指尖向前，眼看右手（圖83、圖84）。

(3) Pivoting on the left forefoot, swing the heel outward.

圖83                                            圖84

Turn the upper body to the right, and the right foot steps to the right front to form the Right Bow Step. Face the right front. Meanwhile, separate both hands; the right hand moves up to eye-level, palm facing upward diagonally; the left hand falls down to the outside of the left hip, palm facing downward, fingers pointing forward. Eyes look at the right hand (Figure 83, Figure 84).

## 【要領】

向右轉體時要沉穩、自然，整個動作連貫、鬆活，方向應偏右30°。

### Key Points

When turning to the right, keep the upper body steady and natural. Keep the entire movement smooth and fluid. Face 30° to the right, when the movement is completed.

## 十九、提　手

左腳前跟半步，身體重心再移於左腿，然後右腳提起落下，腳跟著地，膝部微屈，成右虛步。同時，右掌略向側方斜帶，再向前方下落成側立掌，高與眉齊；左手上提舉於右肘內側，高與胸齊，兩手手心相對，眼看右手（圖85、圖86）。

## 19. Lifting a Hand

The left foot follows up in a half step. Shift the weight onto the left leg. Lift the right heel and bend the knee to form a right Empty Step. Meanwhile, push the right palm outward then in front of the face at eyebrow-height, palm facing the left. Bring the left hand to the inside of the right elbow at chest level. Both palms are facing inward. Eyes look at the right index finger (Figure 85, Figure 86).

### Key Points

The key points are same as former "Lifting a Hand".

圖85                          圖86

84

## 二十、白鶴亮翅

動作與要領均同前「白鶴亮翅」（圖87～圖89）。

## 20. White Crane Spreads Wings

The movements and Key Points are the same as former "White Crane Spreads Wings" (Figure 87 – 89).

圖87

圖88

圖89

## 二十一、左摟膝拗步

動作與要領均與前「左摟膝拗步」相同（圖90～圖93）。

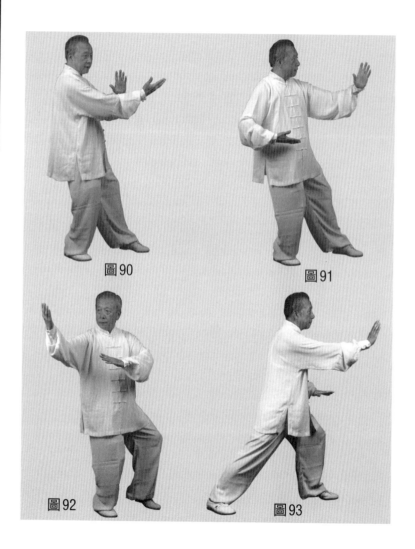

圖90　　　　　　　　圖91

圖92　　　　　　　　圖93

## 21. Brush Knees and Twist Steps—Left

The movements and Key Points are the same as former "Brush Knees and Twist Steps – Left" (Figure 90 – 93).

## 二十二、海底針

右腳向前跟進半步，身體重心再移至右腿；左腳稍向前移步，腳尖點地，成左虛步。同時，身體稍向右轉，右手下落經體前右方向後向上提抽至肩上右耳旁，再隨上體左轉由耳旁斜向前下方插去，掌心向左，指尖斜向下；同時，左手向前向下畫弧落於左胯旁，手心向下，指尖向前，眼看前下方（圖94、圖95）

圖94　　　　　圖95

【要領】

身體要先向右轉，再向左轉。完成此式上體略前傾，但不可低頭，臀部不可外凸，左膝要微屈。

## 22. Needle to Sea Bottom

The right foot follows up in a half step. Shift the weight onto the right leg. The left foot takes a slight step forward with only the toes touching the ground to form an Empty Step. Meanwhile, turn the upper body to the right slightly. The right hand draws an arc upward to the outside of the right ear and thrusts down toward the lower front, palm facing left, fingers pointing downward diagonally. The left hand draws an arc to the lower front up to the outside of the left hip, palm facing down, fingers pointing forward. Eyes look at the lower front (Figure 94, 95).

### Key Points

Turn the upper body to the right first, then the left. When the movement finished, the upper body leans forward no more than 45°. Do not push the buttock out. Do not bow the head. Bend the left knee slightly.

## 二十三、閃通臂

上體稍向右轉，左腳向前邁出，屈膝弓腿成左弓步。同時，右手由體前上提，屈臂上舉，停於額前上方，掌心翻轉斜向上，拇指朝下；左手上提經胸前推出，高與鼻尖平，手心向前，眼看左手（圖96）。

【要領】

完成此式時，上體要自然正直，鬆腰鬆胯。左臂不可全伸直，背部肌肉要展開。推掌、舉掌和弓腿動作三者協調一致，兩腳橫向距離約10公分，不可過寬。

### 23. Flashing the Arm

Turn the upper body to the right slightly. The left foot steps forward to form a Left Bow Step. At the same time, raise the right hand in front of the body, bending the arm, turning it over above the forehead, palm facing the upward diagonally and thumb pointing downward. Raise the left hand in front of the

圖96

chest to push forward and to the left slightly at the nose level, palm facing forward. Eyes look at the left hand (Figure 96).

### Key Points

When the movement is completed, relax the waist and hips; do not extend the left arm straight. Muscles on the back should be stretched. Push the hand should be in coordinated with the movement of raising hand and the Bow Step. The horizontal distance of the feet is about 10 cm; should not be too wide.

## 二十四、轉身撇身捶

1. 重心後倚，右腿慢慢彎曲，身體重心移於右腿，上體右轉，左腳尖裡扣，而後重心再移於左腿。同時，右手隨轉體向右向下變為拳經腹前繞行至左肋旁，拳心向下；左手上舉於頭前上方，臂成半圓形，手心斜向上，眼看前方（圖97）。

### 24. Turn Body and Throw the Fist

(1) Shift the weight backward. Bend the right leg slowly; shift the weight onto the right leg. Turn the upper body to the right and swing the left toes inward. Then shift the weight onto the left leg. Meanwhile, the right hand follows the body and turns into a fist. Move the fist across the abdomen and stop it at the outside of the left ribs, the palm facing downward. Raise the left hand above the forehead, arm ached, palm facing upward

diagonally. Eyes look at the front (Figure 97).

2. 身體繼續右轉，右腳提起向右前邁出，腳尖稍斜向右，變為右弓步。同時，右拳翻轉，拳心向上向前撇出，左手由上而下落於右肘內側，眼看右拳（圖98）。

(2) Turn the upper body to the right. The right foot steps forward with the toes pointing the right front to form a Right Bow Step. Meanwhile, the right fist punches to the upper front with the back of the fist in front of the chest, the palm facing upward. The left hand falls down to the inside of the right elbow. Eyes look at the right fist (Figure 98).

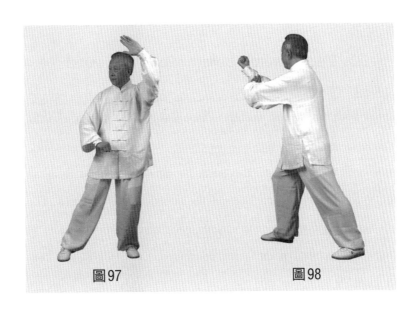

圖97　　　　　　　圖98

右腳先收回（不可點地）再邁出。弓腿和搬拳動作要一致，方向要偏右15°。

**Key Points**

Bring the right foot back first without touching the ground, then step forward. The Bow Step is in coordination with the punch. The direction is 15° to the right.

## 二十五、進步搬攔捶

1. 左腿彎曲，身體重心移於左腿，上體微左轉，右腳收回停於左腳內側，腳尖可點地。同時，右拳翻轉，拳心向下，由前向下經腹前向左畫弧至左肋旁；左臂下落由前向後上方畫弧平屈於胸前，手心向下，眼看前方（圖99）。

### 25. Step forward, Deflect, Parry and Punch

（1）Shift the weight onto the left leg and bend it. Turn the upper body to the left slightly. Place the right foot inside of the left foot, with only the toes touching the ground. Meanwhile, turn over the right fist, the palm facing downward to draw an arc to the lower left and stops at the outside of the left ribs. The left arm draws an arc to the upper back and bends vertically in front of the chest, palm facing downward. Eyes look at the front (Figure 99).

2. 右轉體，右腿向前墊步邁出，腳尖外撇。同時，右拳經胸前向前翻轉撇出，拳心向上；左手由右臂外側落於左胯旁，掌心向下，指尖向前，眼看右拳（圖100）。

（2）Turn the upper body to the right. The right foot steps forward with the toes pointing right front. Meanwhile, the right fist punches downward with the back of the fist in front of the chest, the palm facing upward. The left hand falls down to the outside of the left hip. Eyes look at the right fist (Figure 100).

3. 重心移於右腿，上體右轉，左腳向前邁一步。左手上起，經左側向前上畫弧攔出，手心向前下方；

圖99　　　　　　圖100

同時，右拳向右畫弧收至右腰旁，拳心向上，眼看左手（圖101）。

(3) Shift the weight onto the right leg. Turn the upper body to the right. The left foot steps forward. Move the left hand from the left to the upper front and parry in front of the body, palm facing the lower front. Meanwhile, the right fist draws an arc to the right then backward and stops at the right side of the waist. The palm is facing up. Eyes look at the left hand (Figure 101).

4. 左腿屈膝前弓成左弓步。右拳向前打出，拳眼向上，高與胸平，左手附於右前臂內側，眼看前方（圖102）。

圖101　　　　　　　　　　圖102

（4）Bend the left knee forward to form a Right Bow Step. The right fist punches forward at the chest level, the eye of the fist facing upward. The left palm is inside of the right forearm. Eyes look at the right fist（Figure 102）.

## 【要領】

與前「進步搬攔捶」相同。

## Key Points

Are the same as the former "Step forward, Deflect, Parry and Punch".

# 二十六、上步攬雀尾

1. 身體重心稍向後移，身體半面左轉，左腳尖外撇。同時，左手向下向左後上方畫弧平屈於胸前，手心向下；右拳同時變掌由前向下畫弧停於胸前，手心向上，與左手上下相對，成抱球狀；右腳前進停於左腳內側，腳尖可點地，眼看右手（圖103）。

## 26. Step up and Grasp Bird's Tail

（1）Shift the weight backward slightly. Turn the upper body 90° to the left and swing the left toes outward. Meanwhile, the left hand draws an arc downward then to the back left. Bend the arm in front of the chest, palm facing downward. The right fist turns into an open palm, drawing an arc downward in front

of the chest, palm facing upward. The right hand is corresponding with the left hand as if holding a ball. The right foot steps
forward to the inside of the left foot; toes can be touching the
ground. Eyes look at the right hand (Figure 103).

2. 下面掤、捋、擠、按各法均與圖8～圖17的動
作說明相同（圖104～圖113）。

(2) The rest of the movement is the same as Figure 8 ~
Figure 17. Please refer to (Figure 104 – 113).

【要領】

與前「攬雀尾」相同。

圖103　　　　　　　圖104

圖105

圖106

圖107

圖108

圖109

## Key Points

Are the same as "Grasp Bird' s Tail".

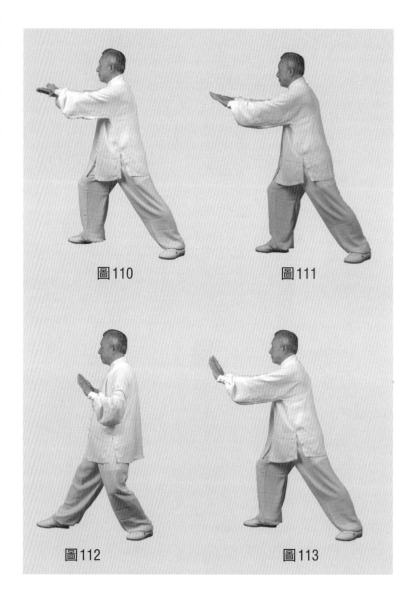

圖110

圖111

圖112

圖113

## 二十七、單　鞭

動作和要領與前「單鞭」相同（圖114～圖118）。

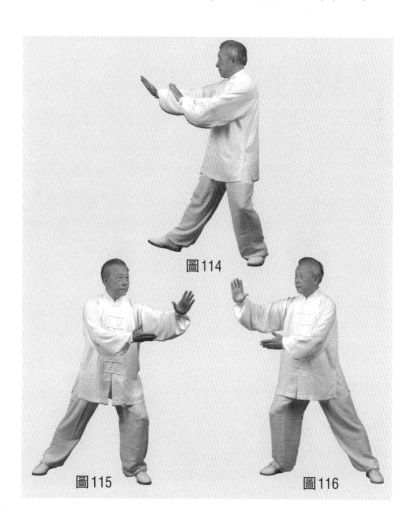

圖114

圖115

圖116

### 27. Single Whip

The movements and Key Points are the same as former "Single Whip" (Figure 114 – 118).

## 二十八、雲　手

1. 身體重心移於右腿，上體漸漸右轉，左腳尖裡扣。左手自腹前向右上畫弧至右肩前，手心斜向後；同時，右勾手變掌，手心向右前，眼看右手（圖119、圖120）。

圖117　　　　　　　圖118

## 28. Cloud Hands

（1）Turn the upper body to the right gradually, shifting the weight onto the right leg, leading the left toes to swing inward. At the same time, the left hand draws an arc downward, then to the right, crossing the front of the abdomen and stops in front of the right shoulder, the palm facing backward diagonally. The right hand changes its hook into an open palm to face the right front. Eyes look at the right hand (Figure 119, Figure 120).

2. 上體慢慢左轉，身體重心隨之逐漸左移。左手由臉前向左側運轉，手心漸漸轉向左方；右手由右下經腹前向左上畫弧至左肩前，手心斜向後。同時，右

圖119　　　　　　圖120

腳左移靠近左腳，成小開立步，兩腳相距10～20公分眼看右手（圖121、圖122）。

(2) Turn the upper body to the left slowly and shift the weight to the left gradually. As the left hand draws an arc past the front of the face to the left, it is turned over to face the left. The right hand draws an arc from the lower right, across abdomen to the upper left and then stops in the front of the left shoulder, palm facing backward diagonally. At the same time, the right foot takes a small step towards the left foot to form Opening Step. The feet are 10～20 cm apart. Eyes look at the right hand (Figure 121, Figure 122).

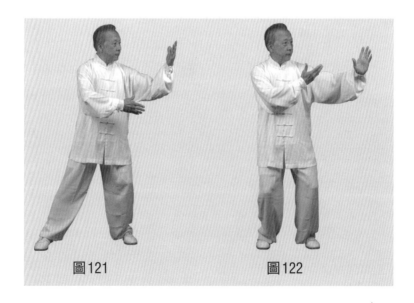

圖121　　　　　　　圖122

3. 上體再向右轉，同時左手經腹前向右上畫弧至右肩前，手心斜向後；右手繼續向右側運轉，手心翻轉向右。隨之左腳向左橫跨一步，眼看左手（圖123、圖124）。

（3）Continue to turn the upper body to the right. Meanwhile, the left hand draws an arc past the abdomen to the upper right and stops in the front of the right shoulder, palm facing backward diagonally. The right hand continues to move to the right and turns over to face the right. The left foot takes a step aside. Eyes look at the left hand (Figure 123, Figure 124).

4. 與動作2說明同（圖125、圖126）。

圖123　　　　　　　　圖124

5. 與動作 3 說明同（圖 127、圖 128）。

6. 與動作 2 說明同（圖 129、圖 130）。

（4）Repeat（2），in the opposite direction（Figure 125, Figure 126）.

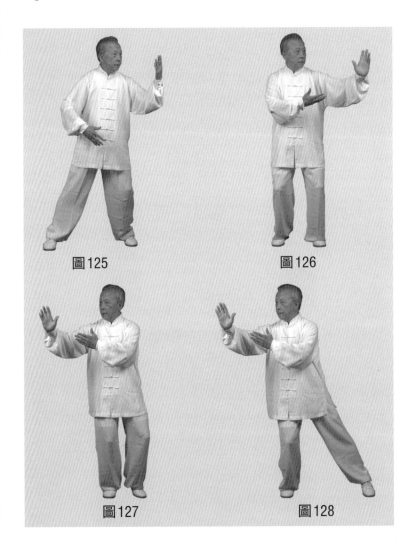

圖 125　　　　　　　　圖 126

圖 127　　　　　　　　圖 128

(5) Repeat (3), in the opposite direction (Figure 127, Figure 128).

(6) Repeat (2), in the opposite direction (Figure 129, Figure 130).

【要領】

雲手轉動要以腰脊為主，鬆腰、鬆胯，上體水平移動，不可忽高忽低。兩臂運轉要隨腰的轉動而動，不可夾腋，要圓活自然，速度勻緩。下肢橫跨步要腳前掌先著地再踏實全腳，要做到點起點落，腳尖向前，兩腳保持平行，不可成八字步。眼睛要隨左右手而移動視線。最後一個雲手，右腳收跟時，腳尖應裡

圖129　　　　　圖130

扣，便於接「單鞭」動作。

## Key Points

Waist and spine lead the upper body turn. Relax waist and hips. Keep the upper body at the same level; do not move it up and down. The moving of the hands is led by the waist; do not close the armpit, which should be rounded and natural. While stepping aside, place the forefoot to the ground first, then the entire foot. There should not be any heavy steps. The feet remain parallel to each other; do not make a " / \ " shape; toes point forwards. Eyes follow the hands. In the last "cloud hand", when the heel is brought back， the right toes should be swung inward， in order to connect to the next movement "Single Whip".

## 二十九、單　鞭

雲手左右共做五個，右手運轉至右上方時變為勾手。同時，左腳邁出變為「單鞭」式。動作過程與前「單鞭」式相同（圖131～圖133）。

### 【要領】

與前「單鞭」式相同。

## 29. Single Whip

The former movement includes five Cloud Hands. When the right hand moves to the upper right, turn it into a hook.

Meanwhile, the left foot steps up to form a Bow Step. The rest of the movement is the same as the former "Single Whip" (Figure 131～ Figure 133).

### Key Points

Are the same as the former "Single Whip".

## 三十、高探馬

1. 右腳跟進半步，上體微向右轉，重心移至右腿。右勾手變成掌，兩手心翻轉向上，肘部微屈。左

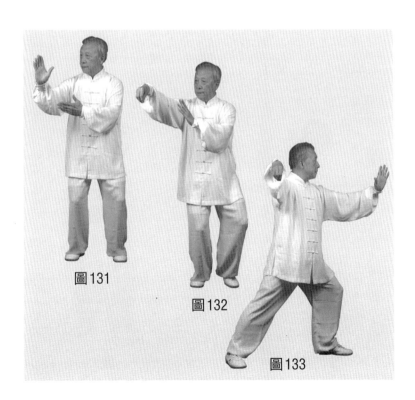

圖131

圖132

圖133

腳跟漸漸離地，眼看左前方（圖134）。

### 30. Patting a High Horse

（1）The right foot follows up in a half step. Shift the weight to the right leg. The right hand changes from a hook into an open palm. Turn over both hands simultaneously to face upward. Raise both arms, elbows bent. Lift the left heel off the ground gradually. Eyes look at the front (Figure 134).

2. 上體稍左轉，面向前方，右掌經右耳旁向前推出，手心向前，手指與眼同高；左手收至左側腰前，手心向上。同時，左腳向前移，腳尖點地，成左虛步，眼看右手（圖135）。

圖134　　　　　　　　　　　圖135

（2）Turn the upper body to face the front and push the right arm from the right ear forward to head level. The palm faces forward, fingers pointing up. The left hand moves to the left side of the waist, palm facing upward, fingers pointing to the right. Meanwhile, lift the left foot and step forward, touching the ground with only the toes to form an Empty Step. Eyes look at the right hand（Figure 135）.

## 【要領】

上身仍然正直，雙肩要下沉，右肘微下垂。跟步移換重心，身體不要起伏，上體也不可前傾。

### Key Points

The upper body is upright; shoulders are sunken; and the right elbow is bent vertically. While stepping forward and shifting the weight, the body should not move up or down; should not move forward or backward.

# 三十一、右分腳

1. 左手手心向上，前伸至右手腕背面，兩手交叉，隨即向兩側分開並向下畫弧，再抱成十字手。同時，左腳向左前方邁出，腳尖略外撇，成左弓步，然後把右腳收到左腳內側，腳尖可點地，眼看右前方（圖136～圖138）

### 31. Separate Legs – Right

(1) Extend forward the left hand over the back of the right wrist to form "X" in front of the chest. The left palm faces upward. Then separate both hands to the sides, then inward to form an "X" again. Meanwhile, step forward with the left foot and swing the toes outward to form "Bow Step". Then place the right foot beside the left foot, with or without the toes touching the ground. Eyes look at the front (Figure 136~138).

2. 兩臂向左右畫弧分開，平舉於身體兩側，肘部微屈，手心均向外。同時，右腿屈膝提起，而後使小腿向前方慢慢踢出，腳面展平，眼看右手（圖139）。

圖136　　　　　　　圖137

（2）Move both hands to the sides of the body, palms facing outward, elbows bending at shoulder level. Lift the right leg, bend the knee and kick forward with force in the lower leg. The foot is stretched. Eyes look at the right hand (Figure 139).

【要領】

要保持重心穩定，不可前俯後仰。兩手分開時，腕部與肩部齊平，沉肩垂肘。分腳時，左腿要微屈支撐，右臂與右腿上下相對，分腳方向偏右30°。分掌與分腳動作要協調一致。

圖138　　　　圖139

### Key Points

Shift the weight completely and maintain steadiness; do not bend the upper body forward or backward. When both hands are separated, the wrists are at shoulder level. When kicking, the left leg bends slightly to support the body. The direction of the kicking is 30° to the right. The right arm is over the right leg. The separating palms and the kicking are synchronized and finished at the same time.

## 三十二、左分腳

1. 右小腿收回，左腿屈膝，右腳向右前方邁出一步，成右弓步，上體半面右轉。左手由左向下經胸前向前伸出，並將手心轉向上，與右手交叉，左上右下，然後兩臂左右分開，自兩側向下畫弧，再相抱成十字手，左手在外，手心均向裡。同時，左腳收到右腳內側，腳尖點地，眼平視左前方（圖140、圖141）。

### 32. Separate Legs—Left

（1）Bring back the right leg and take a step forward. Bend the left knee to form a Right Bow Step. Extend the left hand forward in front of the chest and turn it over to face up, corresponding with the right hand to form an "X". The left hand is over the right one. Then separate both hands outward then downward to form an "X" again. The left hand is on the outside, both palms facing the body. Place the left foot beside the right one with only the toes touching the ground. Eyes look at the front（Figure 140, Figure 141）.

2. 兩臂向左右畫弧分開，雙手舉於身體兩側，肘部微屈，手心向外。同時，左腿屈膝提起，而後小腿慢慢向左前方踢出，腳面展平，眼看左手（圖142）。

圖140

圖141

圖142

(2) Move both forearms to the sides of the body, palms facing outward, elbows bending slightly. At the same time, lift the left leg, bend the knee at the waist level and kick to the left front slowly with the force in the lower leg. The foot is stretched. Eyes look at the left hand (Figure 142).

## 【要領】

與「右分腳」相同，只是左右相反。分腳方向偏左30°。

### Key Points

Are the same as the former "Separate Legs – Right", in the opposite direction. The direction of the kicking is 30° to the left.

## 三十三、轉身左蹬腳

1. 左腳下落於右腳後，腳尖點地。同時，兩手由左右下落收至腹前合抱，左手在裡，手心均向裡，眼看左手（圖143）。

### 33. Turn the Body and Kick with the Left Heel

(1) Place the left foot behind the right one, with only the toes touching the ground. Meanwhile, move both hands down to the lower abdomen to form "X". The left hand is on the inside, the right on the outside. Both palms face the body. Eyes look at the left hand (Figure 143).

2. 以右腳掌為軸，身體向左後轉，左腳隨之扭轉，兩臂慢慢上舉成十字手再向左右畫弧分開平舉於身體兩側，手心向外，肘部微屈。同時，左腿屈膝提起，左腳慢慢向左前方蹬出，眼看左手（圖144、圖145）。

（2）Pivoting on the right forefoot, turn the upper body to the left and the left foot follows. Move both forearms outward simultaneously to form "X" in front of the chest. The left hand is on the inside, the right on the outside, both palms facing

圖143

圖144

圖145

the body. Move the two forearms to the sides of the body, palms facing outward, elbows bending. At the same time, lift the left leg, bending the knee at the waist level and kicking to the left front slowly with the heel. Eyes look at the left hand (Figure 144, Figure 145).

## 【要領】

身體平衡穩定，不俯不仰。兩手分開時，手腕與肩平。蹬腳時，支撐腿要微屈，左腳尖要勾回，腳跟用力，左臂與左腿上下相對。分手與蹬腳要同時完成。

### Key Points

Shift the weight completely, and maintain steadiness; do not bend the body forward or lean backward. When both hands are separated, both wrists are at shoulder level. When kicking, the supporting leg is bent slightly. For the kicking foot, toes point backward, energy delivered to the heel. The left arm is over the left leg. The separating palms and the kick are synchronized and finished at the same time.

## 三十四、左右摟膝拗步

1. 左腿下落，再向左前方邁出，成左弓步。同時，左臂屈肘，左手由上方畫弧落於右肩前，右手心

翻轉向上，然後左手摟左膝停於左胯旁，右手則從右
耳旁向前推出，眼看右手（圖146、圖147）。

### 34. Brush Knees and Twist Steps – Left and Right

（1）The left foot falls down to the left front to form a Left Bow Step. Meanwhile, bend the left arm. The left hand draws an arc to the front of the right shoulder. The right palm turns over to face upward. Then, the left hand moves around the left knee, to stop at the outside of the left hip. Push the right hand from the right ear. Eyes look at the right hand (Figure 146, Figure 147).

2. 右摟膝拗步動作與圖36～圖39說明相同（圖148～圖151）。

圖146　　　　　　　　圖147

（2）The rest of the movement is the same as figure 36～39.
（Figure 148 ～ 151）

圖148

圖149

圖150

圖151

【要領】

同前「左右摟膝拗步」。

Key Points

Are the same as the former "Brush Knees and Twist Steps – Left and Right".

# 三十五、進步栽捶

身體重心略後移，右腳尖外撇，上體右轉。同時，左手隨轉體落於右肩前，右手向後方上舉變拳。而後左腳前進一步，成左弓步。左手摟左膝停於左胯旁，右拳則向前下方栽出，拳心斜向下，拳眼向左，眼看前下方（圖152～圖154）。

【要領】

上體正直，鬆腰、鬆胯，保持肩平。

## 35. Step forward and Punch downward

Shift the weight backward and turn the upper body to the right, swinging the right toes outward. Meanwhile, the left hand follows the upper body in front of the right shoulder. Raise the right hand backward and turn it into a fist. The left foot steps forward to form a Bow Step. Move the left hand around the left knee and stop it beside the left hip. The right fist punches downward in front of the body. The palm faces downward, the eye of the fist facing left. Eyes look downward

（Figure 152 – 154）.

## Key Points

The upper body is upright；the waist and hips are relaxed；shoulders are flat.

## 三十六、翻身白蛇吐信

1. 身體重心後倚，右拳上提，右前臂橫置於胸前，拳心向下，左手自左向前畫弧上舉至頭部前上方。同

圖152

圖153

圖154

時，左腳尖裡扣，上體右轉，重心再移於左腿；右腳先收回再向右後方邁出一小步，腳尖略外撇，身體重心大部在左腿，右膝略屈。右拳在右腳落地的同時向同一方向撇出，拳心向上，肘部下垂，眼看右拳（圖155～圖158）。

## 36. White Snake Turns and Protrudes its Tongue

（1）Shift the weight backward. Lift the right fist and bend the forearm in front of the chest vertically, the palm facing down. The left hand draws an arc from the left to the upper front of the head. Meanwhile, swing the left toes inward; turn the upper body to the right and shift the weight onto the left leg. Bring the right foot back, then take a small step to the

圖155          圖156

back right and swing the toes inward. The most weight is on the left leg. Bend the right knee slightly. While the right foot touching the ground, the right fist punches downward with the back of the fist in the same direction of the right foot, the palm facing upward, the elbow pointing down. Eyes look at the right fist (Figure 155 – 158).

2. 左手經右拳上方向前推出，掌心向前；右拳變掌收至右腰旁，掌心向上。同時，右腿屈膝前弓，成右弓步，眼看左手（圖159）。

（2）Push forward the left hand over the right fist, the palm facing forward. The right fist changes into an open palm

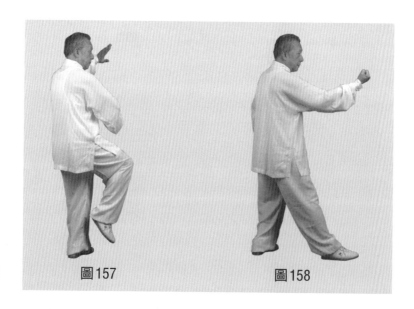

圖157　　　　　　　圖158

and pulls back to the right side of the waist, palm facing up. Meanwhile, bend the right leg forward to form a Right Bow Step. Eyes look at the left hand (Figure 159).

3. 身體重心移於左腿，右腳略後撤，前腳掌著地，成右虛步。同時，右手變拳從左手下方向前打出，拳眼向上，高與胸齊，左掌附於右前臂內側，眼看右拳（圖160）。

(3) Shift the weight onto the left leg. Draw back the right foot slightly with only the toes touching the ground to form an Empty Step. Meanwhile, the right hand turns into a fist and punches to the lower front, beneath the left hand. The eye of

圖159　　　　　　圖160

the fist is facing upward at chest level. The left hand touches the inside of the right forearm lightly. Eyes look at the right fist (Figure 160).

## 【要領】

上體保持正直。左手前推時，要向右向前略帶弧線。右拳打出時，臂不可伸直，要沉肩垂肘。右腳後撤時，要先蹺腳尖，再撤步，要自然平穩。轉身白蛇吐信整體方向偏右約15°。

### Key Points

Maintain an upright upper body. When pushing the left hand, should push it to the right front in an arc. When punching with the back of the fist, do not extend the arm until its straight; sink the shoulder and elbow. When the right foot is taking a step backward, raise the toes first, and then step backward with steadiness. When turning the body and punching down, the direction should be about 15° to the right.

## 三十七、進步搬攔捶

身體左轉，右拳經腹前向下向左上繞行停於腰旁，拳心向下。右腳收回至左腳內側，腳尖可點地。左掌翻轉，手心向上經腹前向左後再向前上繞行，左前臂平屈胸前，掌心變為向下。其餘動作與前「進步搬攔捶」說明相同，即圖47～圖49（圖161～圖164）。

【要領】

與前「進步搬攔捶」相同。

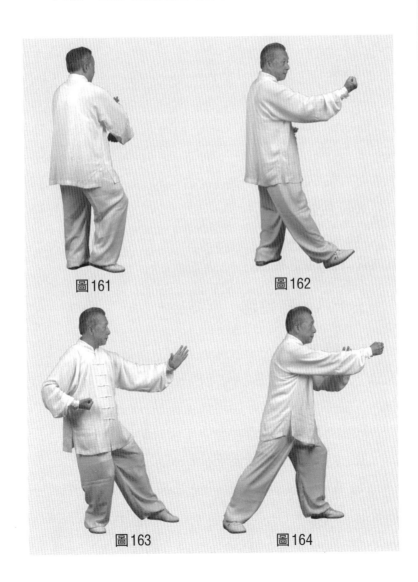

圖161　　　　　　　圖162

圖163　　　　　　　圖164

### 37. Step forward, Deflect, Parry and Punch

Turn the upper body to the left. The right fist moves past the abdomen downward, then to the upper left and stops at the right side of the waist, the palm facing downward. Bring the right foot beside the left foot, with or without the toes touching the ground. Turn over the left palm to face up and move it past the abdomen to the back left, then to the upper front. Bend the left forearm in front of the chest, palm facing downward. The rest of the movement is the same as the former "Step forward, Deflect, Parry and Punch" Figure 47 – 49 (Figure 161 – 164).

### Key Points

The Key Points are the same as the former "Step forward, Deflect, Parry and Punch".

# 三十八、右蹬腳

1. 兩手上舉向左右分開，並向下畫弧，在胸前十字交叉，右手在外，手心均向裡。同時，身體重心略後移，左腳尖稍外撇，身體再移至左腿，右腳跟至左腳內側，腳尖可點地，眼看右前方（圖165、圖166）。

### 38. Kicking with the Right Heel

（1）Move both hands up to the chest to form "X". The left hand is on the inside, the right one outside. Both palms face the body. Meanwhile, shift the weight backward and swing the left toes outward. Then shift the weight onto the left leg. Place the right foot beside the left foot, with or without the toes touching the ground. Eyes look at the right front (Figure 165, Figure 166).

2. 右腿屈膝提起，右腳再慢慢向右前方蹬出，腳尖回勾，腳跟用力。同時，兩手向左右分開，肘微屈，兩臂平舉，眼看右手（圖167）。

圖165

圖166

圖167

(2) Lift the right leg, bend the knee and kick to the right front slowly with the heel; deliver the energy to the heel, toes pointing backward. At the same time, move both hands to the sides of the body, palms facing outward, elbows bending at shoulder level. Eyes look at the right hand (Figure 167).

【要領】

與前「右分腳」相同，只是腳尖回勾，力點在腳跟。

### Key Points

The Key Points are the same as the former "Separate Legs-Right". The only difference: Toes should point backward; deliver the energy to the heel.

## 三十九、左披身伏虎

1. 右腳收回落於左腳後方，成交叉步。同時，左手由左上方向體前繞行，停於右前臂內側，眼看右手（圖168）。

### 39. Cover and Hide a Tiger-Left

(1) Place the right foot behind the left one to form a Crossing Step. Meanwhile, move the left hand from the upper left across the body to the inside of the right forearm. Eyes look at the right hand (Figure 168).

2.左腿提膝，左腳向左側方撤一步，同時上體左後轉，左腿屈膝成左弓步。同時，兩手一起向腹前下落，右手變拳停於左胸前，拳心向下；左手變拳由下向左上畫弧，停在左額上方，拳心向外，兩拳上下相對，眼隨轉體而動，然後平視右前方（圖169）。

（2）Lift the left knee and step to the back left. Turn the upper body to the left. Bend the left knee to form a Left Bow Step. Meanwhile, both hands fall in front of the abdomen simultaneously. The right hand turns into a fist and stops moving in front of the chest, the palm facing downward. The left hand turns into a fist and it is raised above the left of the forehead. The palm is facing outward. The two fists correspond with each

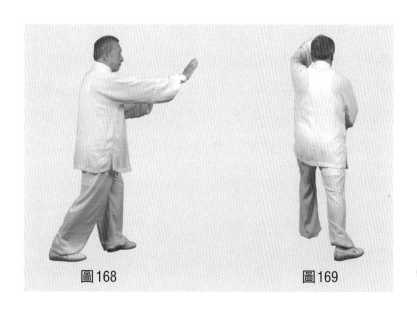

圖168　　　　　圖169

other. Eyes follow the body to look straight ahead（Figure 169）.

## 【要領】

交叉步落腳距離不宜過大，完成動作時，左弓步方向與中軸線垂直。兩臂呈半圓形，胸肌要放鬆。弓步時要鬆腰、落胯。

### Key Points

The crossing feet should not be too far apart. When the movement is completed, the direction of the Bow Step is 90° from the centre of the body. The arms are arched; chest muscles are relaxed; waist is relaxed; hips are sunken.

## 四十、右披身伏虎

身體重心後移，左腳尖裡扣，上體右轉，重心再移至左腿；隨即右腳向右側方邁出一步，弓腿成右弓步。同時，兩拳變掌下落經腹前向右畫弧，左掌變拳停於右胸前，拳心向下；右掌變拳經身體右側上舉於右額上方，拳心向外，兩拳上下相對，眼看左前方（圖170～圖172）。

### 【要領】

除無交叉步外，其餘與「左披身伏虎」相同，只是左右相反，完成方向相反。

## 40. Cover and Hide a Tiger-Right

Shift the weight backward and swing the left toes inward. Turn the upper body to the right and shift the weight onto the left leg. The right foot steps aside; bend the leg to form a Right Bow Step. Meanwhile, turn both fists into open palms and draw an arc to the right across the abdomen. The left hand turns into a fist in front of the chest, the palm facing downward. The right hand turns into a fist passing the right side of the body and raise above the right forehead. The palm is facing outward. The two fists correspond with each other. Eyes look at the left front (Figure 170 – 172).

圖170　　　　圖171　　　　圖172

Key Points

The key points are the same as "Cover and Hide a Tiger–Left" except "crossing step" and in opposite directions.

## 四十一、回身右蹬腳

1. 左膝彎曲，右腳尖裡扣，上體左轉，左腳尖隨之外撇，身體重心移於左腿。左拳隨轉體上舉，兩臂在臉前分開變掌，再合抱於胸前成十字手，右手在外，手心均向裡。同時，右腳收回到左腳內側，腳尖可著地，眼看右前方（圖173～圖175）。

【要領】

上體左轉時，重心在兩腿中間，左腳隨即外撇，

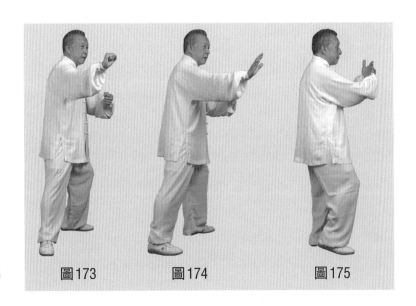

圖173　　　　圖174　　　　圖175

完成此動作要自然平穩。

## 41. Turn the Body and Kick with the Right Heel

（1）Bend the left knee and swing the right toes inward. Turn the upper body to the left and lead the left toes swing outward. Shift the weight onto the left leg. Raise the left fist along the body. Separate both hands in front of the face and turn into open palms. Then move them inward to form an "X" in front of the chest. The right hand on the outside, both palms facing the body. Meanwhile, place the right foot beside the left foot, with or without the toes touch ing the ground. Eyes look at the right front （Figure 173 – 175）.

### Key Points

When turn the upper body to the left, share the weight with both legs then swing the left toes outward. The movement should be completed steadily and naturally.


2. 蹬腳動作與前「右蹬腳」說明相同（圖176）。

【要領】

與前「右分腳」相同，只是腳尖回勾，腳跟著力。

（2）The rest of the movement is the same as the former "Kick with the Right Heel" (Figure 176).

### Key Points

The Key Points are the same as the former "Separate Legs-

Right". The only difference: Toes should point backward and deliver the energy to the heel.

## 四十二、雙峰貫耳

1. 右小腿回收，膝蓋提起。左手由後向上向前落至體前，兩手心翻轉向上，兩手同時向下畫弧分落於右膝兩側，眼看前方（圖177）。

### 42. Striking Ears with Both Fists

（1）Bring back the right lower leg and lift the right knee. Move the left hand to the upper front and stop it in front of the body. Both hands turn over to face upward. Then move both hands downward to the sides of the right thigh. Eyes look at the

圖176　　　　　　　圖177

front（Figure 177）.

2. 右腳向右前方落下，重心漸漸前移，成右弓步，面向右前方。同時，兩掌漸漸變為拳，分別從兩側向上向前畫弧至面部前方，成鉗狀，兩拳相對，與耳同高，兩拳眼均斜向下，兩拳相距約20公分，眼看兩拳前方（圖178、圖179）。

（2）The right foot steps to the right front and shift the weight forward to form a Right Bow Step. The head faces the right front. At the same time, form fists with both hands gradually and punch from either side of the upper body in front of the face to form a " \ / " shape at ear level. Both fists are corre-

圖178　　　　　　圖179

sponding with each other and the eyes of them face downward diagonally; apart is about 20 cm. Eyes look ahead (Figure 178, Figure 179).

## 【要領】

完成動作時頭頸正直，鬆腰，鬆胯，兩拳鬆握，沉肩垂肘，兩臂保持弧形。方向同「回身右蹬腳」一致。

### Key Points

When the movement is completed, keep the head and neck upright; relax the waist and hips; do not hold the fists too tight; sink the shoulders and elbows; keep the arms arched. The direction of the body is the same as "Turn and Kick with the Right Heel".

## 四十三、左蹬腳

1.身體重心後移，右腳尖外撇。兩拳變掌向左右分開，向下畫弧後合抱於胸前成十字手，左手在外，手心均向裡。同時，重心移於右腿，左腳收至右腳內側，腳尖可點地，眼看左前方（圖180、圖181）。

### 43. Kicking with the Left Heel

(1) Shift the weight backward and swing the right toes outward. The both hands turn into open palms and separate them downward to form an "X" in front of the chest. The left is

on the outside, both palms facing the body. Meanwhile, shift the weight onto the right leg; place the left foot beside the right foot, with or without the toes touching the ground. Eyes look at the left front (Figure 180, Figure 181).

2. 兩臂慢慢分開畫弧成左右平舉，肘部微屈，手心向外。同時，左腿提起慢慢向左前方蹬出，腳尖回勾，腳跟用力，眼看右手（圖182）。

（2）Move the two arms to the sides of the body, palms facing outward, elbows bending at shoulder level. At the same time, lift the left leg and kick to the left front slowly with the heel, toes pointing backward, delivering the energy to the heel.

圖180　　　　　　　　　圖181

Eyes look at the right hand (Figure 182).

【要領】

與前「轉身左蹬腳」相同，只是蹬腳方向與中軸線相合。

Key Points

The Key Points are the same as the former "Turn and kick with the Left Heel". The only difference is the direction of the kick.

## 四十四、轉身右蹬腳

1. 左腿屈膝收回向右腿外側落下，趁左腿落勢，以右腳掌為軸，向右後轉體270°，左腳落地後，身體

圖182

重心即刻移於左腿，右腳前掌著地。同時，兩手向左右下落，向下畫弧，再向上合抱於胸前成十字手，右手在外，手心均向裡，眼看右前方（圖183、圖184）。

### 44. Turn the Body and Kick with the Right Heel

（1）Bend the left knee and place the left foot outside the right foot. Pivot on the right forefoot and turn the upper body 270° to the right. After the left foot touching the ground, shift the weight onto the left leg at once. The right foot rests on its forefoot. Meanwhile, separate hands and draw arcs downward to form an "X" in front of the chest. The right hand is on the outside, both palms facing the body. Eyes look at the right front (Figure 183, Figure 184).

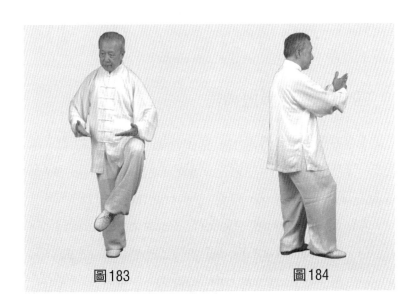

圖183　　　　　　　圖184

2. 兩臂分開向左右平舉，肘部微屈，手心向外。同時，右腿屈膝提起，右腳慢慢向右前方蹬出，腳尖回勾，腳跟用力，眼看右手（圖185）。

（2）Move both hands to the sides of the body, palms facing outward, elbows bending at shoulder level. At the same time, lift the right leg, bend the knee and kick to the right front slowly with the heel, toes pointing backward, delivering the energy to the heel. Eyes look at the right hand (Figure 85).

【要領】

與前「轉身左蹬腳」相同，只是左腳蹬變為右腳蹬，方向與中軸線一致。

Key Points

The Key Points are the same as the former "Turn and kick with the Left Heel", in the opposite direction.

## 四十五、進步搬攔捶

1. 右腳下落向前邁出，腳尖外撇。同時，右掌下落變拳，經腹前向上向前撇出，拳心向上；左掌屈肘收至身體左側，掌心向下，眼看右拳（圖186、圖187）。

### 45. Step forward, Deflect, Parry and Punch

（1）The right foot falls and steps forward. Swing the toes outward. At the same time, the right hand turns into a fist, past the abdomen to punch to the upper front with the back of the fist, the palm facing up. Bend the left elbow to the left side of the body, palm facing downward. Eyes look at the right fist (Figure 186, Figure 187).

2. 其餘動作同前「進步搬攔捶」圖48、圖49說明（圖188、圖189）。

圖185

圖186

圖187

（2）The rest of the movement is the same as the former "Step forward, Deflect, Parry and Punch", referring Figure 48, Figure 49（Figure 188, Figure 189）.

## 【要領】

與前「進步搬攔捶」相同。

### Key Points

The key Points are the same as former "Step forward, Deflect, Parry and Punch".

## 四十六、如封似閉

動作與要領均與前「如封似閉」相同（圖190～

圖188　　　　圖189

圖193）。

## 46. Withdraw and Push

The movements and Key Points are the same as former "Apparent Close" (Figure 190 – 193).

圖190

圖191

圖192

圖193

## 四十七、十字手

動作與要領均與前「十字手」相同（圖194〜圖197）。

圖194　　　　　　　　　圖195

圖196　　　　　　　　　圖197

## 47. Cross Hands

The movements and Key Points are the same as former "Cross Hands" (Figure 194 – 197).

第四組

## 四十八、抱虎歸山

動作和要領均與前「抱虎歸山」相同（圖198、圖199）。

圖198

圖199

## 48. Hold a Tiger back to the Hill

The movements and Key Points are the same as former "Hold a Tiger back to the Hill"(Figure 198, Figure 199).

## 四十九、斜攬雀尾

動作和要領均與前「斜攬雀尾」相同（圖200～圖205）。

## 49. Grasp Bird's Tail Diagonally

The movements and Key Points are the same as former "Grasp Bird's Tail Diagonally"（Figure 200 – 205）.

圖200                    圖201

## 五十、橫單鞭

動作和要領與前「單鞭」相同。只是左腳應向起

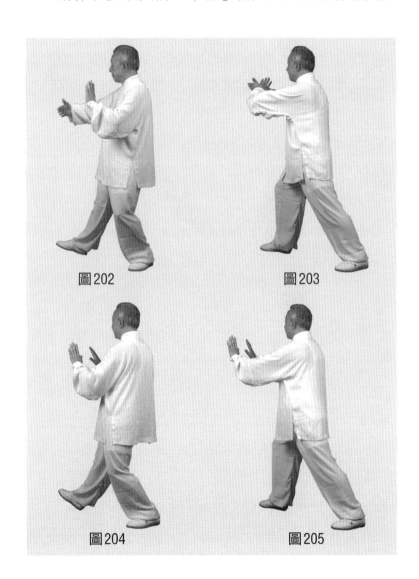

圖202                圖203

圖204                圖205

式方向邁出，並落地成左弓步，方位與中軸線垂直，
與起式方向一致（圖206～圖209）。

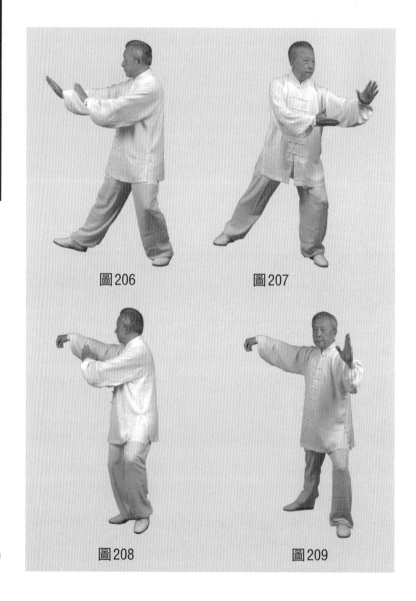

圖206

圖207

圖208

圖209

## 50. Cross Single Whip

The movements and Key Points are the same as former "Cross Single Whip". The only different is: the right foot should step to the direction of the "Opening" form and the "Bow Step" (Figure 206 – 209).

# 五十一、左右野馬分鬃

1. 身體重心微微移至左腳，同時身體微向左方轉動。左臂平屈於胸前，右勾手變掌經體前向左前下方畫弧至與左手相對成抱球狀，左手心向下，高與胸平；右手心向上，高與腰平。同時，右腳跟進至左腳內側，腳尖可點地，眼看左手（圖210）。

## 51. Splitting Wild Horse's Mane—Left and Right

（1）Shift the weight onto the left leg and slightly turn the upper body to the left. Bend the left arm in front of the chest. The right hand changes the hook into an open palm and draws an arc to the left front in corresponding with the left hand as if holding a ball. The left hand faces downward at chest level; the right hand faces upward at the waist level. Meanwhile, bring the right foot in and place it beside the left foot. For beginners, toes can touch the ground for stability. Eyes look at the left hand (Figure 210).

2. 上體微右轉，右腳向右前方邁出，左腳跟後蹬，左腿伸直，成右弓步。同時，上體右轉不停，兩手隨轉體慢慢分開，右手向上，左手向下，右手高與眼平，手心斜向上，肘微屈；左手落於左胯旁，肘亦微屈，手心向下，指尖向前，眼看右手（圖211）。

（2）Turn the upper body to the right slightly. The right foot steps to the right front and push the ground with the heel to extend the leg to form a Right Bow Step. At the same time, continue to turn the upper body to the right, both hands follow the body and separate, the right one goes upward to the eye level, palm facing upward diagonally, bending the elbow; the left one goes downward to the outside of the left hip, bending the

圖210　　　　　圖211　　　　　圖212

elbow slightly, palm facing downward, fingers pointing forward. Eyes look at the right hand (Figure 211).

3. 上體略後移，右腳尖蹺起微向外撇約45°，隨後腳掌踏實，右腿前弓，上體右轉，重心移於右腿。同時，右手翻掌向下，右臂收於胸前平屈；左手經體前向右畫弧放在右手下方，兩手相抱成球狀。左腳隨即收至右腳內側，腳尖可點地，眼看右手（圖212～圖214）。

(3) Turn the upper body backward slightly. Pivot on the right heel outward 45°, then place the entire foot on the ground firmly. Bend the right leg forward, shift the weight onto the

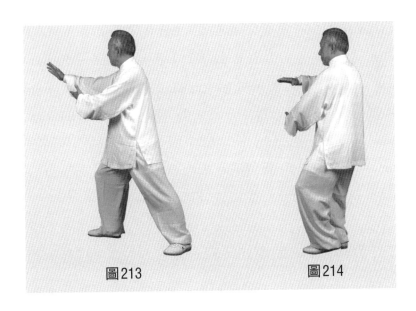

圖213　　　　　　　　圖214

right leg. Meanwhile, turn over the right palm to face downward and bend the arm in front of the chest vertically. The left hand draws an arc to the right across the body and places under of the right hand as if holding a ball. Bring the left foot in and place it beside the right foot. For beginners, toes can touch the ground for stability. Eyes look at the right hand (Figure 212 – 214).

4. 左腳向左前邁出，左腿屈膝前弓，右腿自然伸直，成左弓步。同時，上體左轉，兩手隨轉體分別向左上、右下分開，左手高與眼平，手心斜向上，肘微屈；右手落在右胯旁，手心向下，肘亦微屈，眼看左手（圖215）。

（4）The right foot steps to the left front, bending the knee and extending the right leg to form a Left Bow Step. At the same time, turn the upper body to the left, both hands follow the body and separate, the left hand goes upward to the eye level, palm facing upward diagonally, bending the elbow slightly; the right hand goes downward to the outside of the right hip, bending the elbow slightly, palm facing downward, fingers pointing forward. Eyes look at the left hand (Figure 215).

5. 與動作3說明同，只是左右相反（圖216～圖218）。

6. 與動作4說明同，只是左右相反（圖219）。

（5）Repeat（3），in the opposite direction（Figure 216 – 218）.

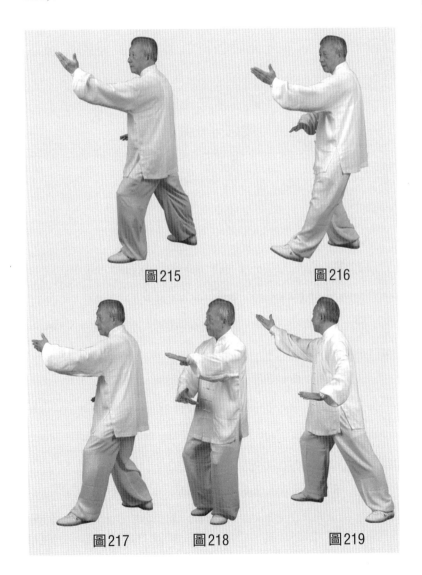

圖215　　　　　　　圖216

圖217　　　圖218　　　　圖219

（6）Repeat（4）, in the opposite direction （Figure 219）.

【要領】

（1）上體保持正直平穩，不可前俯後仰，胸部寬鬆舒展。兩臂分開時保持弧形。上體轉動以腰為軸。

（2）弓步時，兩腳橫向距離不超過30公分。弓步與分手動作的速度要均勻一致。

（3）分手時，上臂有向外分靠的意念，另一手有下採之意。弓步邁步時要輕靈平穩，不可「砸夯」步。

## Key Points

（1）Maintain the upper body upright; do not bend the upper body forward or backward; keep the chest relaxed and comfortable. Separate arms in arc. The upper body follows the waist to turn around.

（2）For the Bow Step, feet should rest on sides of the center of the body and stand on two parallel lines separately, which should be no more than 30cm apart. The feet and hands move in the same and even speed.

（3）When separating the hands, the upper hand acts pushing outward; the lower hand acts pushing downward. Move feet gently and fast. Always lift the heel or forefeet first, and place the palm or heel to the ground first. Do not make a heavy step.

## 五十二、進步攬雀尾

1. 上體後坐，重心移於左腿，右腳尖蹺起微向外撇，隨即右腿前弓，身體右轉，重心移於右腿。同時，右手翻轉，手心向下收於胸前，右臂平屈，左手經腹前向右畫弧放在右手下，兩手心相對成抱球狀。左腳跟步至右腳內側，腳尖可點地，眼看右手（圖220～圖222）。

### 52. Step forward and Grasp Bird's Tail

（1）Shift the upper body backward slightly. Shift the weight

圖220　　　圖221　　　圖222

onto the left leg. Raise and swing the right toes outward. Bend the right leg forward, turn the body to the right, and shift the weight onto the right leg. Meanwhile, the right hand turns over to face downward in front of the chest; the left hand draws an arc, across the abdomen to the right and stops under the right hand, in corresponding with the right hand as if holding a ball. The left foot follows up to the side of the right foot; toes can be touching the ground. Eyes look at the right hand (Figure 220 – 222).

2. 左腳向左前方邁出，成左弓步。同時，左臂向左前方掤出，手高與肩平；右手向右向下落於右胯旁，手心向下，眼看左前臂（圖223）。

圖223

（2）The left foot steps forward to form a Left Bow Step. Meanwhile, the left forearm pushes to the left front; hand is at shoulder level. The right hand falls down to the lower right, and stop outside of the right hip, palm facing downward. Eyes look at the left forearm（Figure 223）.

3. 上體後坐，左腳尖外撇，身體左轉。同時，左手翻掌向下，臂平屈胸前，右手經腹前畫弧與左手成抱球狀。右腳跟步至左腳內側，腳尖可點地，眼看左手（圖224、圖225）。

（3）Shift the upper body backward. Raise and swing the left toes outward. Turn the body to the left. Meanwhile, the left

圖224　　　　　　　　圖225

hand turns over to face downward, bending the arm in front of the chest; the right hand draws an arc, across the abdomen to the left and stops under the left hand, in corresponding with the left hand as if holding a ball. The right foot follows up to the side the left foot; toes can be touching the ground. Eyes look at the left hand (Figure 224 – Figure 225).

4. 其餘動作和要領均與前「上步攬雀尾」相同（圖226～圖234）。

(4) The rest of the movement and Key Points are the same as the former "Step up and Grasp Bird's Tail" (Figure 226 – 234).

圖226                         圖227

圖228

圖229

圖230

圖231

圖232

## 五十三、單　鞭

動作和要領均與前「單鞭」相同（圖235～圖239）。

圖233

圖234

圖235

圖236

## 53. Single Whip

The movements and Key Points are the same as former "Single Whip"(Figure 235 – 239).

圖237

圖238                圖239

88
式
太
極
拳
套
路
動
作
詳
解

161

## 五十四、左右穿梭（四斜角）

1. 身體重心略向後移，左腳尖裡扣，上體右後轉，身體重心移於右腿，右腳掌為軸腳跟內轉，兩腿成半坐盤勢。同時，右勾手變掌，前臂平屈於胸前，手心向下；左手由左向下畫弧停在腹前，手心向上，兩手心相對成抱球狀。

然後左腳向左前方邁出一步，成左弓步。左手翻掌由臉前向上舉架，置於左額前，手心斜向上；右手則向前方推出，高與鼻尖平，眼看右手（圖240～圖242）。

圖240

圖241

圖242

## 54. Working with a Shuttle(4 Diagonal directions)

（1）Shift the weight backward and swing the left toes inward. Turn the upper body to the right and shift the weight onto the right leg. Pivot on the right forefoot and swing the toes inward. Both legs are in a half squat. Meanwhile, turn the right hand from the hook into an open palm and bend the forearm in front of the chest vertically, palm facing downward. Move the left hand downward in front of the abdomen, palm facing upward. Both hands are placed as if holding a ball.

The left foot steps to the left front to form a Left Bow Step. Turn over the left hand in front of the face and raise it over the left of the forehead, palm facing upward diagonally. The right hand pushes forward at nose level. Eyes look at the right hand（Figure 240 – 242）.


2. 身體重心移於右腿，左腳尖裡扣，上體右後轉，重心再移於左腿，右腳收至左腳裡側，前腳掌著地。同時，左手下落，前臂平屈於胸前；右手下落在腹前，手心向上，與左手相對成抱球狀。

然後左腳裡扣，或腳跟後碾，身體向右後轉，右腳向右前方邁出一步，屈膝前弓成右弓步。右手上舉置於右額前，手心斜向上，左手則向前推出，眼看左手（圖243～圖245）。

(2) Shift the weight onto the right leg and swing the left toes inward. Turn the upper body to the back right and shift the weight onto the left leg. Bring the right foot beside the left foot with only the forefoot touching the ground. Meanwhile, the left hand falls and bend the forearm in front of the chest vertically, palm facing downward. Move the right hand downward in front of the abdomen, palm facing upward. The two hands are corresponding with each other as if holding a ball.

Swing the left toes inward or the heel outward. Turn the body to the back right. The right foot steps to the right front to form a Right Bow Step. Raise the right hand over the right forehead, palm facing upward diagonally. The left hand

圖243　　　　圖244　　　　圖245

pushes forward at nose level. Eyes look at the left hand
（Figure 243 – 245）.

3. 身體重心稍向後移，右腳尖微外撇，隨之身體
重心移於右腿，左腳收至右腳內側，腳尖可點地。左
手畫弧收至腹前，手心向上；右手下落，右前臂經胸
前時手心向下與左手相對成抱球狀。隨之左腳向左前
方邁出一步，成左弓步。左手弧線上舉於左額前，手
心斜向上，右手則畫弧線向前推出，眼看右手（圖
246、圖247）。

（3）Shift the weight backward and swing the right toes
outward. Shift the weight onto the right leg. Bring the left foot

圖246                    圖247

beside the right foot with or without the toes touching the ground. The right hand falls down and the forearm bends in front of the chest, palm facing downward. Move the left hand down in front of the abdomen, palm facing upward. Both hands are corresponding with each other as if holding a ball. Then the left foot steps to the left front to form a Left Bow Step. Raise the left hand over the left forehead, palm facing upward diagonally. The right hand pushes forward at nose level. Eyes look at the right hand (Figure 246, Figure 247).

4. 重心移向右腿，左腳尖裡扣，上體右後轉，右腳收至左腳內側，腳尖點地。同時，左手下落，手心向下，前臂平屈；右手畫弧收至腹前，與左手成抱球狀。

然後左腳裡扣，上體繼續右後轉，右腳向右前方邁出一步，成右弓步。同時，右手上舉於右額前，手心斜向上，左手弧形向前推出，眼看左手（圖248～圖250）。

(4) Shift the weight onto the right leg and swing the left toes inward. Turn the upper body to the back right and shift the weight onto the left leg. Bring the right foot beside the left foot with only the toes touching the ground. Meanwhile, the left hand falls and the forearm bends in front of the chest vertical-

ly, palm facing the downward. Move the right hand downward in front of the abdomen, palm facing upward. The two hands are corresponding with each other as if holding a ball.

Then swing the left toes inward. Turn the body to the back right. The right foot steps to the right front and form a Right Bow Step. Meanwhile, raise the right hand over the right forehead, palm facing upward diagonally. The left hand pushes forward at nose level. Eyes look at the left hand (Figure 248 – 250).

【要領】

上體保持正直，手向上舉架時，不可聳肩、抬肘；前推掌與鬆腰弓腿應協調一致。弓步時，兩腳橫

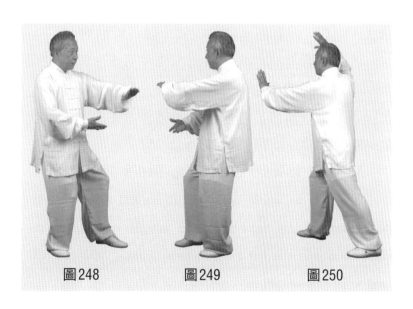

圖248　　　　圖249　　　　圖250

向距離要在 30 公分之內，左右穿梭為面向四個斜角，與中軸坐標成「米」字形。

### Key Points

Keep the upper body upright; do not bend forward. When raising the hand over the forehead, do not raise the shoulder and the elbow. The hand push is coordinated with the relaxing of the waist. For the Bow Step, the horizontal distance of both feet is no more than 30 cm. The directions of the movement are four diagonal directions.

## 五十五、進步攬雀尾

1.重心後移，右腳尖微外撇，隨之重心前移於右腿。左手心翻轉向上，右手心轉向下，兩手相對成抱球狀。同時，左腳跟至右腳內側，腳尖可點地。

然後左腳再向左前方邁出，成左弓步。同時，兩手左上右下分開，左前臂向前掤出，高與肩平，手心向裡；右手下落放於右胯旁，肘微屈，手心向下，指尖向前，眼看左前臂（圖251、圖252）。

### 55. Step forward and Grasp Bird's Tail

（1）Shift the weight backward. Raise and swing the right toes outward slightly. Shift the weight onto the right leg. Meanwhile, turn over the left hand to face upward, turn the right hand to face downward in corresponding with the left hand as if holding a ball. The left foot follows up to the side of the right foot; toes can be touching the ground.

The left foot steps to the left front forming a Left Bow Step. Meanwhile, separate both hands; the left forearm pushes to the left front; hand is at shoulder level. The right hand falls down to the lower right and stops at the outside of the right hip, palm facing downward. Eyes look at the left forearm (Figure 251, Figure 252).

2.上體重心稍向後移，左腳尖外撇，上體左轉，右腳收至左腳內側，腳尖可點地。同時，左臂平屈胸前，右手經體前向左畫弧與左手上下相對成抱球狀，

圖251　　　　　圖252　　　　　圖253

169

眼看左手（圖253）。

(2) Shift the upper body backward. Raise and swing the left toes outward. Turn the body to the left. Meanwhile, turn over the left hand to face downward and bend the arm in front of the chest; the left hand draws an arc, across the abdomen to the right and stops under the right hand, in corresponding with the right hand as if holding a ball. The right foot follows up to the side of the left foot; toes can be touching the ground. Eyes look at the left hand (Figure 253).

3. 其餘動作和要領均與前「上步攬雀尾」相同（圖254～圖262）。

圖254　　　　　　圖255

圖256

圖257

圖258

圖259

圖260

(3) The rest of the movement and Key Points are the same as the former "Step up and Grasp Bird's Tail" (Figure 254 – 262)

## 五十六、單　鞭

動作和要領均與前「單鞭」相同（圖263～圖267）。

圖261

圖262

圖263

## 56. Single Whip

The movements and Key Points are the same as former "Single Whip" (Figure 263 – 267).

圖264

圖265

圖266

圖267

## 五十七、雲　手；五十八、單　鞭

　　動作和要領均與前「雲手」和「單鞭」相同。雲手數量也為5個（圖268～圖282）。

圖268

圖269

圖270

圖271

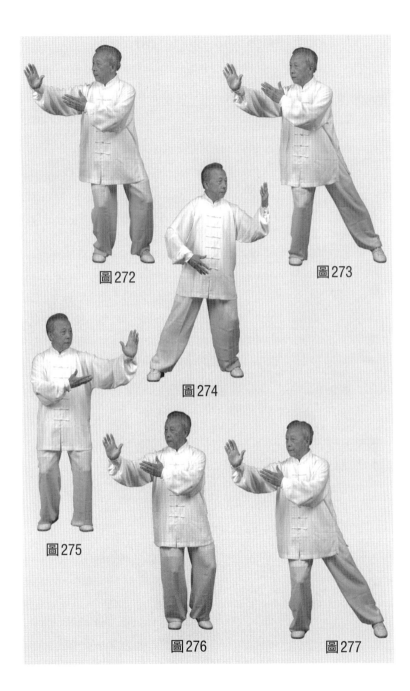

圖272

圖273

圖274

圖275

圖276

圖277

## 57. Cloud Hands, 58. Single Whip

The movements and Key Points are the same as former "Single Whip" and "Cloud Hands" (Figure 268 – 282).

圖278    圖279    圖280

圖281    圖282

# 五十九、下　勢

上體右轉，右腳尖稍外撇，重心移至右腿，右腿屈膝下蹲；左腳以掌為軸，腳跟外蹬，左腿平鋪伸直，成左仆步。同時，左手隨上體轉動向上向右下收至右肩前，然後下沉，掌心轉向外，順左腿內側向前穿出；右勾手在身體右方平舉，勾尖向下，眼看左手（圖283、圖284）。

【要領】

下蹲仆步要根據自身情況決定姿勢高低。左腳尖也可裡扣，但兩腳必須全腳掌著地。上體不可過於前俯。

圖284

圖283

## 59. Push down the Body

Turn the upper body to the right. Swing the right toes outward. Shift the weight to the right leg. Squat with the right leg and pivot on the left forefoot, push the heel outward and stretch the left leg straight to form a Crouch Step. At the same time, the left hand follows the body to move to the upper right and stops in front of the right shoulder. Then move it down along the left leg, palm facing outward. Change the right hand into a hook and raise it to the right of the body, the hook pointing downward. Eyes look at the left hand (Figure 283, Figure 284).

## Key Points

When squatting with the right leg, it depends on the physical condition of the individual to be lower or higher; toes can be swung inward. The upper body should not lean forward too much. Both feet are planted on the ground firmly.

# 六十、左右金雞獨立

1. 左腳尖外撇，右腿漸漸蹬直，上體向前直起，右腳尖裡扣，左腿前弓，身體重心漸漸移至左腿，然後右腿提起成左獨立步。同時，右勾手變掌，沿身體右側向前向上舉起，停於右腿上方，手與鼻平，肘與膝相對，手心向左；左手則下落停於左胯旁，手心向下，眼看右手（圖285、圖286）。

## 60. Golden Cock Stands on One Leg-Left and Right

(1) Swing the left toes outward. Extend the right leg. Stand up and turn the upper body to face the front. Swing the right toes inward. Bend the left leg forward and shift the weight to the right leg gradually. Lift the right leg to form an Independent Step. Meanwhile, change the right hand into an open palm and move it from the right to the upper front and stop above the right leg at nose level, palm facing left, elbow above the right knee. The left hand falls slowly to the outside the left hip, palm facing downward. Eyes look at the right hand (Figure 285, Figure 286).

2. 右腳下落於左腳後，腳尖稍外撇，左腿提起成右獨立步。同時，左掌由下向前舉挑，高與鼻平，肘與膝相對，手心向右；右手下落於右胯側，手心向下，眼看左手（圖287）。

(2) Place the right foot behind the left foot and swing the toes outward slightly. Lift the left leg to form an Independent Step. Meanwhile, raise the left hand at nose level, palm facing right, elbow above the left knee. The right hand falls slowly to the outside the right hip, palm facing downward. Eyes look at the left hand (Figure 287).

【要領】

獨立步支撐腿要稍彎曲，不可挺直。上體要正直，獨立步要平穩。

Key Points

The supporting leg should be bent slightly without rigidness. When raising the legs, keep the upper body upright and steady.

## 六十一、左右倒捲肱

1. 上體微右轉，右手回撤並翻掌，手心向上，隨即屈肘，上體微向左轉，手掌經右耳旁向前推出；左手後撤至左肋外側，手心向上。同時，左腳向左後側

圖285　　　圖286　　　圖287

方退一步，身體重心後移，前腳以腳掌為軸扭直，成
右虛步，眼看前方（圖288、圖289）。

## 61. Backward Steps and Swirling Arms—Left and Right

（1）Turn the upper body to the right slightly. Pull back and turn the right hand over to face upward, bending the elbow. Turn the upper body to the left slightly. Push the right hand forward from the ear. Pull the left hand back to the outside of the left ribs, palm facing upward. Meanwhile, the left foot steps to the back left. Shift the weight backward. Pivot on the right forefoot to make the toes pointing forward and form an Empty Step. Eyes look at the front（Figure 288, Figure 289）.

圖288　　　　　圖289

2. 其餘動作和要領均與前「左右倒捲肱」相同（圖290～圖295）。

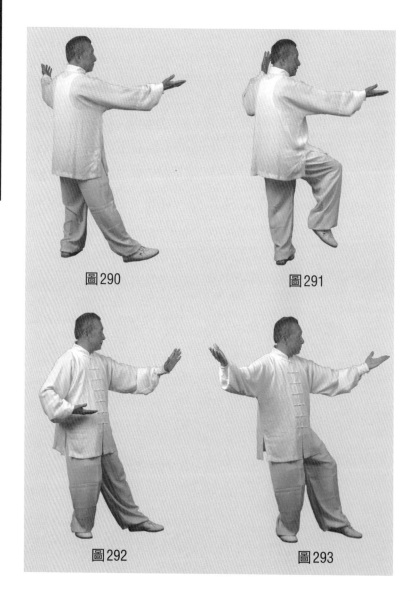

圖290

圖291

圖292

圖293

（2）The rest of the movement and Key Points are the same as the former "Backward Steps and Swirling Arms – Left and Right"（Figure 290 – 295）.

## 六十二、斜飛式；六十三、提手；六十四、白鶴亮翅；六十五、左摟膝拗步；六十六、海底針；六十七、閃通臂；六十八、轉身撇身捶；六十九、進步搬攔捶；七十、上步攬雀尾

這九個拳勢動作和要點均與圖81～圖113各式相同（圖296～圖327）。

圖294　　　　　　　　圖295

圖296

圖297

圖298

圖299

圖300

圖301

88式太極拳 學與練

圖302

圖303

圖304

圖305

圖306

圖307

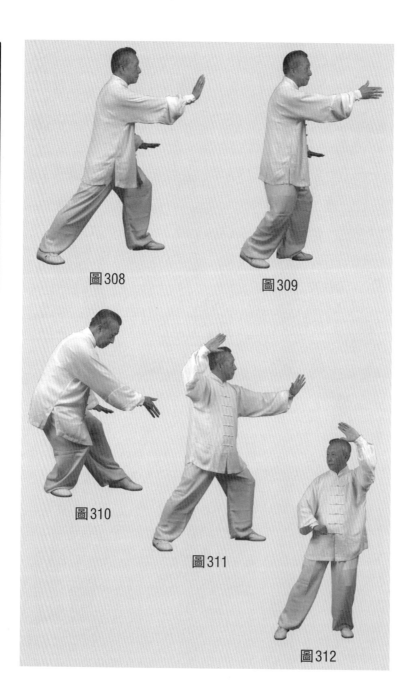

圖308

圖309

圖310

圖311

圖312

圖313　　　　　圖314　　　　　圖315

圖316

圖318

圖317

圖319

圖320

圖321

圖322

圖323

62. Flying Diagonally

63. Lift a Hand

64. White Crane Spreads Wings

圖324

圖325

圖326

圖327

65. Brush Knees and Twist Steps – Left
66. Needle to Sea Bottom
67. Flashing the Arm
68. Turn the Body and Throw Fist
69. Step forward, Deflect, Parry and Punch
70. Step forward and Grasp Bird's Tail

The above 9 movements and Key points are the same as the Figure 81 ～Figure 113（Figure 296 – Figure 327）.

## 第六組

## 七十一、單鞭；七十二、雲手；七十三、單鞭；七十四、高探馬

這四個拳勢動作均與圖 144～圖 135 各式相同（圖 328～圖 349）

## Group 6

71. Single Whip
72. Cloud Hands
73. Single Whip
74. Patting a High Horse

The above 4 movements and Key Points are the same as the Figure 114～Figure 135（Figure 328 – 349）.

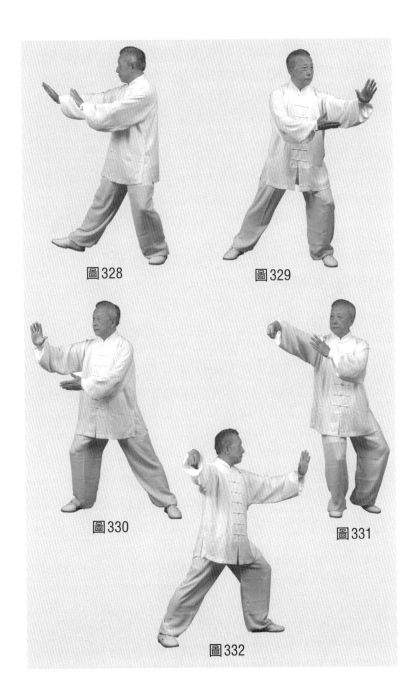

圖328

圖329

圖330

圖331

圖332

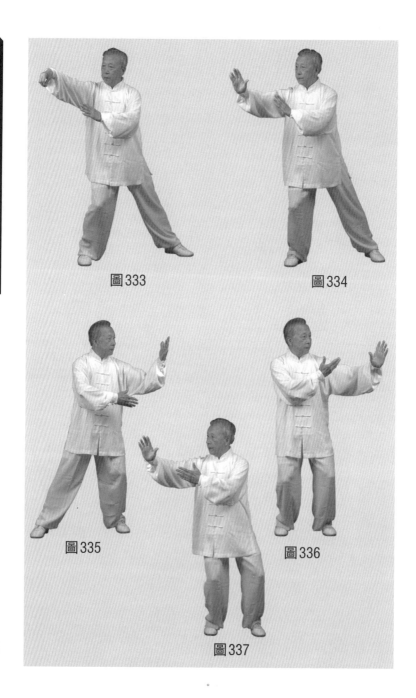

圖333

圖334

圖335

圖336

圖337

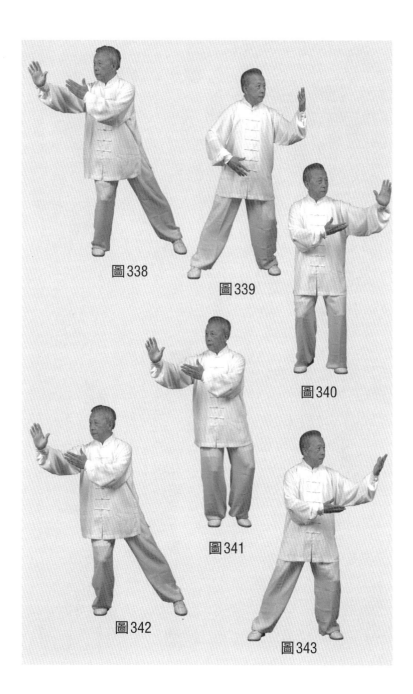

圖338

圖339

圖340

圖341

圖342

圖343

圖344

圖345

圖346

圖347

圖348

圖349

## 七十五、左穿掌

右手稍下落，左手經右手背上方穿出伸向前上方，手心斜向上，高與眼平；右手落於左肘下方，手心向下。同時，左腳向前邁出半步，成左弓步，眼看左手（圖350）。

【要領】

穿伸掌、弓腿、鬆腰要一致。

### 75. Thrust the Left Hand

The right hand falls down a little. The left hand thrust to the upper front passing the right hand's back, palm facing upward diagonally at eye-height. The right hand is under the left elbow,

圖350

palm facing downward. Meanwhile, the left foot steps forward a half step to form a Left Bow Step. Eyes look at the left hand (Figure 350).

### Key Points

The hand thrusts in coordination with the motion of the leg and the waist.

## 七十六、轉身十字蹬腳

重心移於右腿，左腳尖裡扣，上體向左後轉動，重心再移於左腿，右腳跟離地，慢慢提膝。同時，兩手合抱胸前，右手在外，手心均向裡，成十字手。

然後兩手左右分開，手心轉向外。右腳向前方蹬出，眼看右手（圖351～圖353）。

【要領】

獨立時，支撐腿微屈，上體要穩定，右腿要蹬平，腳尖勾回，腳跟用力，腳向正前方。

### 76. Turn the Body and Cross Kick with a Heel

Shift the weight onto the right leg and swing the toes inward. Turn the upper body to the back left and shift the weight onto the left leg. Lift the right knee slowly with the heel off the ground first, then the entire foot. At the same time, both hands form an "X" in front of the chest. The right hand is on the outside. Both hands face the body.

Then separate both hands, palms facing outward. The right foot kicks forward with the heel. Eyes look at the right hand （Figure 351 – 353）.

### Key Points

The supporting leg should be bent slightly without rigidness. Keep the upper body steady. Extend the right leg so that it is parallel to the ground, toes pointing to the back. Deliver

圖351

圖352

圖353

the energy to the right heel. The heel faces the front.

## 七十七、摟膝打捶

右腳在體前下落，腳尖外撇，踏實，上體右轉。同時，右手變拳下落收至右腰側，拳心向上；左手上舉畫弧，屈臂於右胸前，掌心向下，指尖向後。

然後上體左轉，左腳向前邁出一步，成左弓步。左手則從左膝前摟過，停於左胯旁；右拳向前打出，高與腹平，拳眼向上，眼看前方（圖354、圖355）。

【要領】

上體保持正直，鬆腰鬆胯，右拳打出時，右臂不可伸直。

圖354                                    圖355

## 77. Brush Knees and Punch

The right foot falls down in front of the body. Swing the toes outward. Place the entire foot on the ground. Turn the upper body to the right. The right hand turns into a fist at the right side of the waist, the palm facing up. Raise the left hand to draw an arc and bend the arm at the right side of the chest, palm facing downward, fingers pointing backward.

Then, turn the upper body to the left. The left foot steps forward to form a Left Bow Step. The left hand moves across the left knee and stops at the left side of the hip. The right fist punches out at the abdomen level, the eye of the fist facing upward. Eyes look at the front (Figure 354, Figure 355).

### Key Points

Maintain an upright upper body; hips and waist relaxed. The right arm should not be too straight while punching out.

# 七十八、上步攬雀尾

1.重心稍後移，左腳尖外撇，上體左轉。同時，右拳變掌收至腹前，手心向上；左手向左後方再向上畫弧，與右手相抱，左上右下成抱球狀。同時，右腳跟步至左腳內側，腳尖可點地，眼看左手（圖356、圖357）。

## 78. Step forward and Grasp Bird's Tail

(1) Shift the weight backward slightly. Swing the left toes

outward. Turn the upper body to the left. At the same time, the right fist turns into an open palm and pull it back in front of the abdomen, palm facing upward. The left hand draws an arc to the back left corresponding with the right hand as if holding a ball. Meanwhile, the right foot follows up to the side the left foot; toes can be touching the ground. Eyes look at the left hand (Figure 356, Figure 357).

2. 其餘動作和要領均與前「上步攬雀尾」相同（圖358～圖366）。

圖356

圖357

圖358

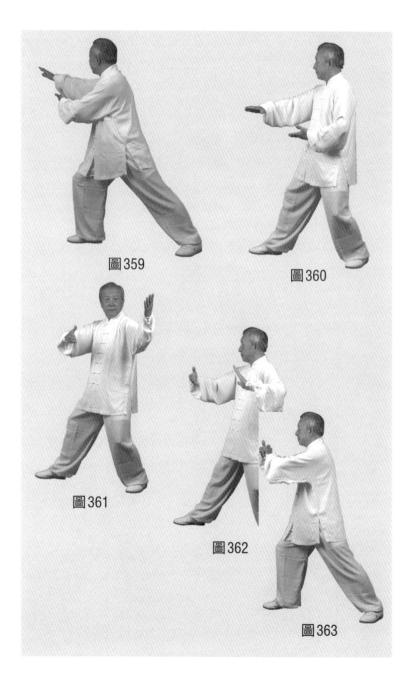

圖359

圖360

圖361

圖362

圖363

(2) The rest of the movement and Key Points are the same as the former "Step up and Grasp Bird's Tail" (Figure 358 – 366).

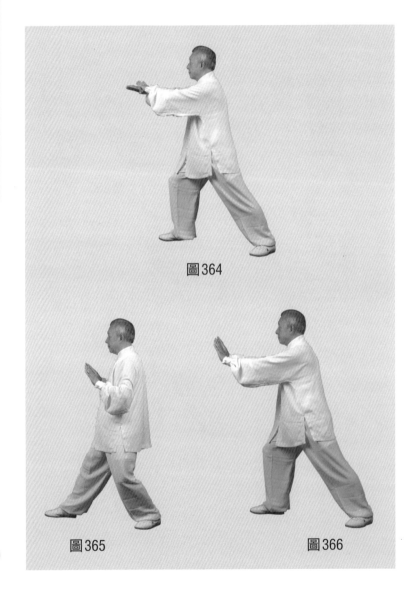

圖364

圖365                    圖366

## 七十九、單　鞭

動作和要領均與前「單鞭」相同（圖367～圖371）。

圖367

圖368

圖369

圖370

## 79. Single Whip

The movements and Key Points are the same as former "Single Whip" (Figure 367 – Figure 371).

## 八十、下　勢

動作和要領均與前「下勢」相同（圖372、圖373）。

## 80. Push down the Body

The movements and Key Points are the same as former "Push down the Body" (Figure 372, Figure 373).

## 八十一、上步七星

左腳尖向外撇，身體重心向左腿移動，身體起

圖371　　　　　　　　　　圖372

立，右腳向前邁出半步，腳尖點地，成右虛步。同時，右手向下向前畫弧，兩手變拳在胸前相互交叉成十字拳，右拳在外，拳心向前，左拳拳心向後，眼向前看（圖374）。

【要領】

兩拳相交，腕部相貼，兩臂圓滿，肌肉放鬆。

## 81. Step forward to Form Seven Stars

Swing the left toes out. Shift the weight onto the left leg and stand up. The right foot takes a half step forward with only the toes touching the ground to form an Empty Step. Meanwhile, the right hand draws an arc downward and forward. Change both hands to fists and meet in front of the chest to

圖373　　　　圖374

form an "X". The right fist is on the outside, palm facing outward.
The left fist is on the inside, palm facing the body. Eyes look
at the front (Figure 374).

### Key Points

The two arms intersect at the wrists; both arms are
arched; muscles are relaxed.

## 八十二、退步跨虎

右腳後撤一步，同時兩拳變掌向下向左右分開，
右手向上畫弧停於右額前方，掌心斜向上；左手下落
停於腰部左前側，掌心斜向外下。身體重心落於右
腿，左腳尖點地，成左虛步，眼看前方（圖375）。

### 【要領】

肩平、胯正，胸部要放鬆，左腿膝部微屈，兩掌
外撐。

### 82. Step back and Ride a Tiger

The right foot takes a step backward. At the same time,
turn the fists into open palms and separate them. The right
hand draws an arc to the front right of the head, palm facing
upward diagonally. The left hand stops at the left front of the
waist, palm facing down and outward. The weight is on the
right leg. The left toes touch the ground to form an Empty Step.
Eyes look at the front (Figure 375).

Key Points

The shoulders are flat; the hips are upright; the chest is relaxed; the left knee is bent slightly. Both palms push outward.

## 八十三、轉身擺蓮

1. 以左腳掌為軸，腳跟外轉，右腳以腳跟為軸，腳尖外撇，身體向右後轉180°，左腳隨轉體向前邁出一步，成左弓步。同時，左手翻轉，手心向上，經左腰側自右手腕上穿出，高與眼平，指尖斜向上；右手則落於左肘下，手心向下，眼看左手（圖376、圖377）。

### 83. Turn the Body with Lotus Kick

（1）Pivot on the left forefoot and swing the heel outward.

圖375　　圖376　　圖377

Simultaneously, pivot on the right heel and swing the toes outward. Turn the body 180° to the right. The left foot follows the body and steps forward to form a Left Bow Step. Meanwhile, turn the left hand over to face upward and thrust it forward from the left side of the waist over the upper side of the right wrist at eye level, fingers pointing upward diagonally. The right hand falls under the left elbow and faces downward. Eyes look at the left hand (Figure 376, Figure 377).

2. 重心後移，上體繼續右轉，左腳尖裡扣，重心再移回左腿；然後右腳提起，由左向右上方擺出，腿要自然伸直。同時，右手順左臂外側上舉，兩手經頭上方先向右後向左側擺過，雙手左手先右手後拍擊右腳面，眼看兩手（圖378～圖380）。

(2) Shift the weight backward and continue to turn the upper body to the right. Swing the left toes inward and shift the weight onto the left leg. Lift the right leg and swing from the left to the upper right, extending the leg naturally. Meanwhile, move both hands to the left first, then across in front of the head to the right and then to the left to pat on the right foot with first the left hand, then the right. Eyes look at both hands (Figure 379 – 380).

## 【要領】

左穿掌方向為前進方向中軸線左後方斜角，即起勢向南，此為西北。擺蓮時，右腿上舉，上體微向前迎，但不可緊張向前彎腰。如身體條件不備，也可不拍腳。

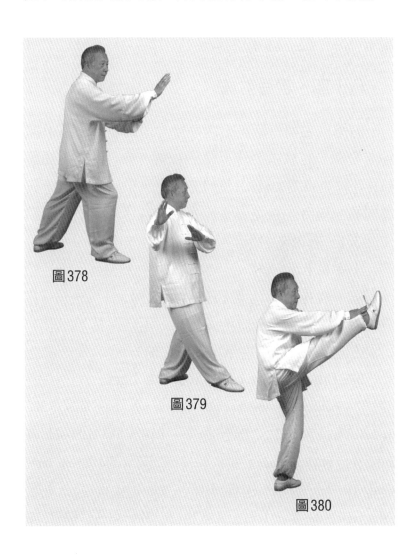

圖378

圖379

圖380

## Key Points

The direction of the thrust is 135° in relation to the direction of the Opening Form. When swinging the foot, raise the right leg and the upper body leans forward slightly; do not bow at the waist. If the physical condition does not allow it, the pat on the foot is not needed.

## 八十四、彎弓射虎

右腳向右前方落步,兩手自身前向右後方弧形擺動並變拳,右拳由後轉至頭部右側,拳心向外,高與額角平;左拳經臉前由左前方打出,拳心斜向前,與鼻同高。同時,右腿屈膝前弓,成右弓步,眼看左拳(圖381～圖383)。

### 【要領】

兩手後擺時,上體和頭要隨之轉動。眼先向右看,再看左拳。定勢時上體正直,兩臂保持半圓形。弓步方向為右前方,左拳方向為左前方。

### 84. Draw a Bow and Shoot the Tiger

The right foot steps forward. Both hands draw arcs to the back left and form fists. The right fist stops at the right side of the head, slightly higher than the eyebrow, palm facing outward. The left fist passes the face to punch to the front left, palm facing the front left at nose height. Meanwhile, bend the right knee to form a Right Bow Step. Eyes look at the left fist (Figure 381 – 383).

### Key Points

When both hands move backward, the upper body and head should follow them. Eyes look at the right first, then the left fist. After settling, the upper body is upright; both arms are arched. The direction of the Bow Step is the right front, while the left fist punches to the left front.

圖381

圖382

圖383

1. 重心向左腿移動，右腳尖裡扣，上體左轉，左腳隨轉體腳尖外撇，隨即右腳收至左腳內側，腳尖可點地。同時，右拳隨轉體向前向左下方弧形下落於左肋前，拳心向下；左拳變掌，手心向上，下落回收，在身體左側畫弧，手心也由向上轉成向下，停於胸前（圖384、圖385）。

## 85. Step forward, Deflect, Parry and Punch

（1）Shift the weight onto the left leg. Swing the right toes inward. Turn the upper body to the left. The left foot follows the body to swing outward. Bring the right foot beside the left one with only the toes touching the ground. At the same time, the right fist draws an arc to the lower left and stops in front of the left ribs. The palm faces downward. The left fist turns into an open palm to face upward and falls down to the left side of the body; turn the palm over to face downward and stops in front of the chest (Figure 384, 385).

2. 其餘動作和要領和圖47、圖48、圖49相同（圖386～圖388）。

（2）The rest of the movement and Key Points are the same as the former "Step forward, Deflect, Parry and Punch"

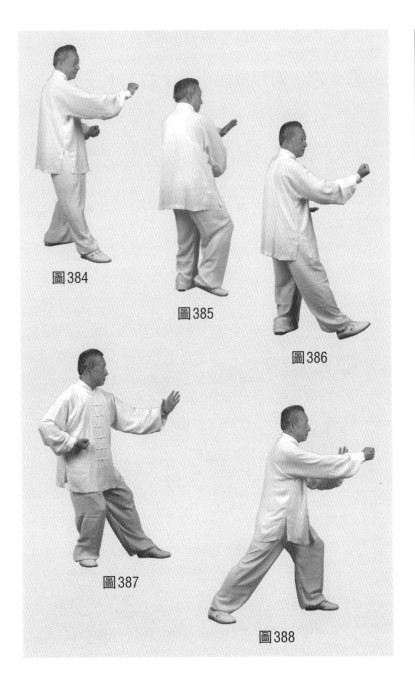

圖384

圖385

圖386

圖387

圖388

Figure 47, Figure 48, Figure 49（Figure 386 – 388）.

## 八十六、如封似閉；八十七、十字手

動作和要領和圖50～圖57相同（圖389～圖396）。

### 86. Withdraw and Push, 87. Cross Hands

The above movements and Key Points are the same as the former "Withdraw and Push" and "Cross Hands" Figure 50 – 57（Figure 389 – 396）.

圖389

圖390

圖391

圖392

圖393

圖394

圖395

圖396

## 八十八、收式還原

　　兩手掌心轉向外，左右分開，與肩同寬，手心向下慢慢下落於兩腿外側；全身放鬆，眼向前看；然後左腳向右腳靠攏，立正還原（圖397～圖400）。

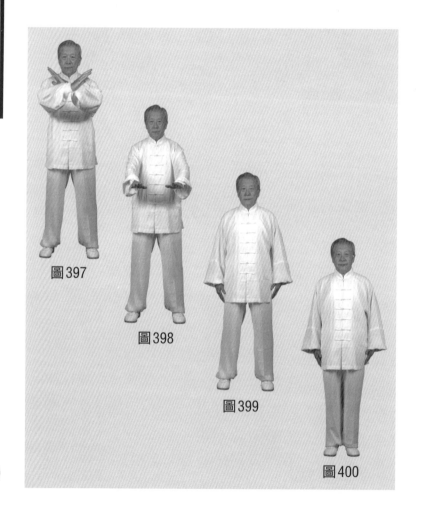

圖397

圖398

圖399

圖400

## 【要領】

兩手下落時，氣要徐徐向下沉，加長呼氣，待呼吸平穩後再收左腳。

還原後應緩慢走動，不做激烈活動。

## 88. Closing

Turn both hands outward and separate them to be apart at shoulders' width. Both hands face downward. Drop the arms slowly to the sides of the body. The entire body is relaxed. Eyes look straight ahead. Bring in the left foot gently and place it next to the right foot. Stand up in the "Preparing" position (Figure 397 – 400).

### Key Points

When arms falling down, take a long and slow breath through the abdomen. After the breath, bring the left foot in gently.

After completing the full form, take a slow walk; do not rush to an intense motion.

# 導引養生功

全系列為彩色圖解附教學光碟

### 張廣德養生著作　每冊定價350元

定價350元

定價350元

定價350元

定價350元

定價350元

定價350元

定價350元

定價350元

定價350元

定價350元

# 輕鬆學武術

定價250元

定價250元

定價250元

定價250元

定價250元

定價250元

定價250元

定價250元

定價280元

定價330元

# 太極跤

定價300元

定價280元

定價350元

# 彩色圖解太極武術

定價220元

定價220元

定價220元

定價220元

定價350元

定價350元

定價350元

定價350元

定價350元

定價350元

定價350元

定價350元

定價350元

定價220元

定價220元

定價220元

定價350元

定價220元

定價350元

定價350元

定價220元

定價220元

定價220元

# 養生保健　古今養生保健法　強身健體增加身體免疫力

 醫療養生氣功　定價250元
 中國氣功圖譜　定價250元
 少林醫療氣功精粹　定價250元
 龍形實用氣功　定價220元
 魚戲增視強身氣功　定價220元
 道家玄牝氣功　定價200元
 仙家秘傳袪病功　定價160元

 少林十大健身功　定價180元
 中國自控氣功　定價250元
 醫療防癌氣功　定價250元
 醫療強身氣功　定價250元
 醫療點穴氣功　定價250元
 中國八卦如意功　定價180元
 正宗易體營養氣功　定價420元

 道家筋經內丹功　定價300元
 三元開慧功　定價250元
 防癌治癌新氣功　定價180元
 喬定興傢家氣功修煉　定價200元
 顛倒之術　定價360元
 簡明氣功辭典　定價360元
 八卦三合功　定價230元

 朱砂掌健身養生功　定價250元
 抗老功　定價230元
 意氣按穴排濁自療法　定價250元
 健身袪病小功法　定價200元
 張氏太極混元功　定價250元
 中國少林禪密功　定價200元
 郭林新氣功　定價400元

 太極　定價280元
 現代原始氣功　定價400元
 開脈太極　定價300元
 溫盤功　定價300元
 太極內功養生法　定價180元
 無極養生氣功　定價200元
 小周天健康法　定價200元

 易筋經　定價350元
 洗髓經　定價400元
 精功易筋經　定價200元
 武當周門七心活氣功　定價280元
 平衡健身法　定價200元
 養生導引術　定價180元
 養生長壽功　定價200元

 太極拳內功養生心法　定價280元
 意拳　定價280元
 靜坐要訣　定價200元

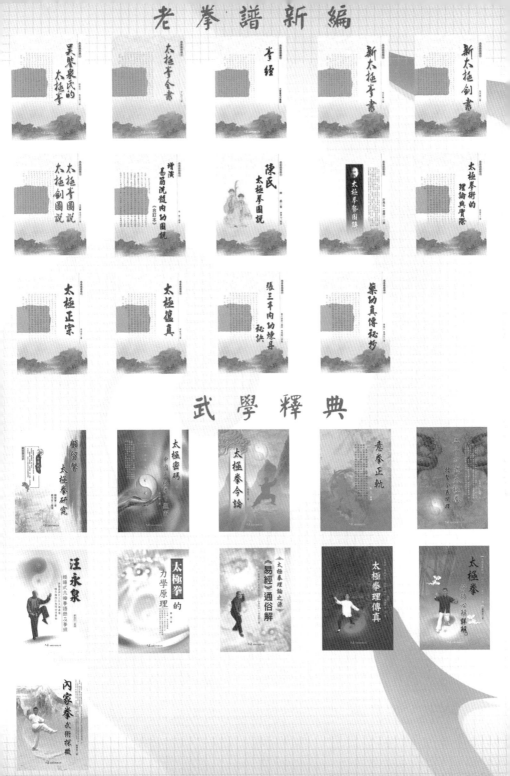

# 太極武術教學光碟

# 歡迎至本公司購買書籍

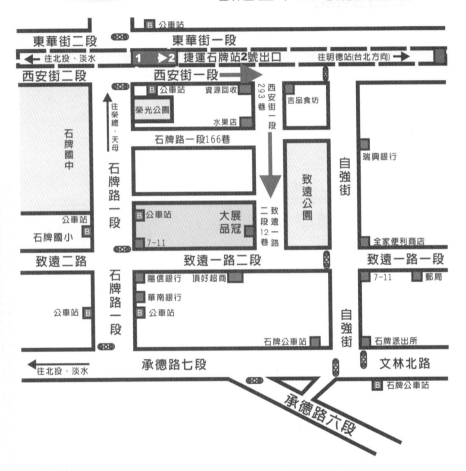

建議路線

1. 搭乘捷運‧公車

　　淡水線石牌捷運站下車，由石牌捷運站 2 號出口出站(出站後靠右邊)，沿著捷運高架往台北方向走(往明德站方向)，其街名為西安街，約走100公尺(勿超過紅綠燈)，由西安街一段293巷進來(巷口有一公車站牌，站名為自強街口)，本公司位於致遠公園對面。搭公車者請於石牌站(石牌派出所)下車，走進自強街，遇致遠路口左轉，右手邊第一條巷子即為本社位置。

2. 自行開車或騎車

　　由承德路接石牌路，看到陽信銀行右轉，此條即為致遠一路二段，在遇到自強街(紅綠燈)前的巷子(致遠公園)左轉，即可看到本公司招牌。

國家圖書館出版品預行編目資料

88式太極拳學與練 ／ 李壽堂　編著
——初版，——臺北市，大展，2014〔民103 . 11〕
面；21公分 ——（中英文對照武學；3）
ISBN　978－986－346－044－2（平裝；附影音光碟）
1.太極拳
528.972　　　　　　　　　　　　　　　　103018039

# 88式太極拳學與練 附 VCD

編　　著／李壽堂
校　　訂／張連友
責任編輯／王躍平　　張東黎
發 行 人／蔡森明
出 版 者／大展出版社有限公司
社　　址／台北市北投區（石牌）致遠一路2段12巷1號
電　　話／（02）28236031・28236033・28233123
傳　　眞／（02）28272069
郵政劃撥／01669551
網　　址／www.dah-jaan.com.tw
E－mail ／ service@dah-jaan.com.tw
登 記 證／局版臺業字第2171號
承 印 者／傳興印刷有限公司
裝　　訂／承安裝訂有限公司
排 版 者／弘益電腦排版有限公司
授 權 者／山西科學技術出版社
初版1刷／2014年（民103年）11月

定　價／300元

大展好書　好書大展
品嘗好書　冠群可期